The
MERE MORTAL'S
Guide to
FINE
DINING

The
MERE MORTAL'S
Guide to
FINE
DINING

from **SALAD FORKS** *to* **SOMMELIERS,**
how to **EAT** *and* **DRINK** *in style*
without **FEAR** *of* **FAUX PAS**

COLLEEN RUSH

BROADWAY BOOKS
New York

PUBLISHED BY BROADWAY BOOKS

Copyright © 2006 by Colleen Rush

All Rights Reserved

Published in the United States by Broadway Books, an imprint of The Doubleday Broadway Publishing Group, a division of Random House Inc., New York. www.broadwaybooks.com

BROADWAY BOOKS and its logo, a letter B bisected on the diagonal, are trademarks of Random House, Inc.

Book design by Mauna Eichner
Illustrations by David Cain

Library of Congress Cataloging-in-Publication Data

Rush, Colleen.
     The mere mortal's guide to fine dining : from salad forks to sommeliers, how to eat and drink in style without fear of faux pas / Colleen Rush.
        p.   cm.
     1. Cookery. I. Title.

TX714.R86 2006
641.5—dc22

2005051223

ISBN-10: 0-7679-2203-4
ISBN-13: 978-0-7679-2203-6

PRINTED IN THE UNITED STATES OF AMERICA

10 9 8 7 6 5 4 3 2 1

First Edition

To Chris, for Jean Georges, Sunday tacos,
sushi, tapas, oysters, and
countless food adventures to come

CONTENTS

INTRODUCTION

Picture it if you will: Christmas Day, 2002, New York City. I am standing at the corner of 60th Street and Central Park West with my very significant other. We are on the threshold of Jean Georges, one of the snazziest and most expensive restaurants in Manhattan. I have waited (and waited) for an occasion that would justify a meal of such extravagance, such expense. Our pending move is the perfect excuse. This is our last blowout meal as residents of New York City. Snow is falling, blanketing the grime that lies beneath the powdery whiteness. Everything is surreally perfect, just as I imagined this moment would be. Except . . . I am suddenly nervous about eating in such a chichi restaurant. I am convinced that *they*—the excessively polished and polite staff—will refuse to let us in. The host will take one look at us and shoo us away with a sniff and a half-raised eyebrow. Or, we will be shuffled off to a table far, far away and our waiter will hate us because we mispronounce *foie gras* and can barely afford the cheapest bottle of wine on the list. I will feel like a bona fide hayseed if I butter my bread the wrong way or use the wrong fork. *They* will see right through us, I think. *We* are not worthy.

I had what I now know to be a common fine dining condition: Fancy-Pants Restaurant Panic. For many a Mere Mortal, fine dining creates needless anxiety about things like whether you're using your knife the right way or where to put your napkin when you leave the table. As I walked through the weighty glass doors of Jean

Georges, my excited anticipation of the meal withered into nervous angst over details. Should we tip the guy who carries our wineglass from the bar to the table? How do we pick a bottle of wine from a list the size of a phone book? Will people stare if I swap a piece of salmon for a nibble of my date's braised beef cheek? Where did that spoon come from and, God help me, what am I supposed to do with it? The *food* was sublime, but the *meal* was nerve-racking because I didn't have all of the tools to fully enjoy the experience.

Like walking into the Met or the Guggenheim, strolling into a swanky dining room has a way of making most of us feel out of place and unsophisticated. Whether you are puzzling over Bordeaux vintages or Mona Lisa's smile, feeling like an uncultured clod punctures the thrill of the experience. Maybe you nod and smile a little too much. Or you wonder if you put the napkin in your lap too soon. You pretend to read the wine list (but really only scan the price list). You agonize over ordering a French dish because you will mangle the pronunciation, and fear the waiter will roll his eyes or guffaw at your ignorance. In no time, you are totally preoccupied by the fact that You. Just. Don't. Get. It. You spend so much of the meal worrying about looking naive and being swindled or committing some heinous etiquette disaster that you wind up overlooking the best part of the meal: eating a multicourse masterpiece.

More than a simple etiquette guide, this book was born of my own formidable shortcomings in fine dining—moments when confusion and doubt steered me into overpriced bottles of wine, mysterious dishes like sweetbreads (which aren't sweet *or* bread), and needless worry about sneering, contemptuous waiters. And I know I'm not alone. Whether you've fumbled through one too many formal business or social dinners or you simply want to explore the world of luxury cuisine, everything you need to feel comfortable and knowledgeable in the realm of fine dining is here: Nitty-gritty details, like the difference between a porterhouse and a T-bone, where your bread plate is, and how to send back a funky bottle of wine. The history of table manners and the mystery of place settings. Practical stuff about ordering wine that will make people think you know more than you do. How to schmooze restaurant staff and read a French menu. This is no pinkies-up, prissy handbook of good manners. It is your practical guide to enjoying, indulging, and feeling utterly competent in any fancy-pants restaurant, from the *amuse-bouche* to dessert. Bon appétit!

If you're ever at a loss for conversation in a stodgy restaurant, these nuggets of information, which pop up throughout the book, will enlighten any meal.

LAGNIAPPE (lahn-YAHP) is a Spanish-French-Creole fusion of a word that means "a little something extra." For the Mere Mortal, it's a bonus dose of dining tips.

EAT THIS is a morsel of oddball food trivia and other useless but fascinating fine dining facts.

TALES OF THE FEAST is a random bit of fine dining and food history, superstition, or custom.

BE A BUFF is a list of reference guides and books recommended for in-depth coverage of topics in each chapter.

1

RELAX—HELP IS ON THE WAY

SCHMOOZING *the* **STAFF** *like a* **SEASONED DINER**

The first rule of mastering fine dining: Get over yourself. An overdeveloped or fragile ego does nothing but interfere with a fantastic meal. You're not alone if you feel intimidated or overwhelmed when you walk into those sumptuous dining rooms or divinely minimalist food meccas, but being cagey or aloof will only make you feel more out of place. The more open and honest you are about what you know—or don't know, as the case may be—the more you will learn, enjoy, and feel at ease in these restaurants.

First and foremost, because the restaurant's staff is trying to deliver this experience to you, you need to know who they are and how to work with them. Despite any fears you may have about stiff maître d's or condescending waiters, generally, the higher the caliber of the restaurant, the better the service. Like all great artists and craftsmen, the culinary crews in fine dining establishments take a tremendous amount of pride in what they do and what they know. But the restaurant-diner relationship is a two-way street. If you have a bad attitude or skulk into a restaurant expecting loads of attitude from the staff, you may indeed get a free helping of attitude with your meal. Show your genuine appreciation and interest, or even cluelessness—by asking questions, encouraging suggestions, and complimenting the staff's efforts—and you will have an extraordinary experience. Restaurant staff love to strut their stuff, and they will go out of their way to dazzle inquisitive and polite diners.

From the maître d'hôtel and sommelier to the garde-manger, whether they're behind the scenes or flitting around your table, getting to know the players in a restaurant is as easy—and as useful—as chatting up the neighbors or your mailman. Yes, many of these people have official Frenchy job titles that are ripe for mispronouncing. They're still just people whose jobs happen to revolve around making you happy and helping you spend your money, some of which ends up in their pockets. All you need to know and do is right here: who they are, what they do, how to pronounce their tongue-twisting titles, and, of course, Mere Mortal, how to become that elite diner: The Regular.

At Your Service: Who's Who in a Restaurant

FRONT-OF-THE-HOUSE STAFF

Reservationists not only take your reservation, they can make all of the little extras happen, like saving that special corner table for you or giving the kitchen advance notice that you're on a gluten-free diet. The person on the other end of the phone wields more power than you think. This is not a nameless, faceless automaton paid to do your bidding, so be calm, cool, and friendly when you call to make a reservation.

How to Suck Up to the Reservationist

Step 1: Know (and use) the reservationist's name. Asking for a name and inserting it when you greet and thank the reservationist is not only common courtesy, it gives you good mojo. If you're trying to get the best table in the house or weasel a reservation when the restaurant is booked, proper name-calling makes you seem more familiar and friendly to the person you're trying to schmooze. It says, "Not only do you know me. You *liiiike* me."

Step 2: Let the compliments fly. Don't hesitate to give a shout-out to a favorite waiter, say how much you love the restaurant, or mention that you picked the restaurant because you're celebrating a special occasion. A brief caution: Reservationists are well trained in sleazy human behavior, so faux flattery will get you nowhere. They've heard it all and know every sob story, ass-kissing compliment, and name-dropping trick in the book.

> **Do say:**
>
> "I love your (insert restaurant's signature dish)."
>
> "My friends rave about the wine list."
>
> "Is Ralph working on Friday? I'd love to sit at one of his tables."
>
> "It's our tenth anniversary, and this is our favorite restaurant in the city."
>
> **Don't say:**
>
> "I'm a friend of the general manager."
>
> "I just love the chef's show on the Food Network! *BAM!*"
>
> "I've never been to the restaurant. Can't you squeeze me in?"
>
> "There's a three-month wait list? The food must be good, huh?"
>
> "I'll have to sell a kidney to pay for this. It better be good."

Step 3: Be informative. Don't wait until you arrive to tell the host or maître d' that you want a table far away from the noisy bar or smoking section, or that your adherence to feng shui principles requires that you have a north-facing booth, or that you'll be dining with a lacto-ovo vegetarian. It's not only okay to spell out any special needs you have, it's a surefire way to get on a restaurant's good side. This information helps the restaurant map out a plan for assigning and turning over tables ahead of time, instead of scrambling to accommodate you when you stroll in.

"People think it's high maintenance to make special requests with the reservationist. If you're celebrating an anniversary or have a special dietary need, or even if it's 'I don't like sitting near sunlight,' we love to know those things ahead of time. The more information you give us, the easier it is for us to make you happy."

TRACEY SPILLANE, general manager, Spago, Los Angeles

LAGNIAPPE

Even if they say they're booked, some restaurants reserve one or two tables for walk-ins, but they rarely advertise it. If you have good rapport, politely ask the reservationist about their policy or, better yet, when to show up for the best shot at a table.

Hosts are the people who greet you at the door and usher you to your table, but they may do double duty as reservationists. They also coordinate the flow of diners and arrange seating in the restaurant as tables turn over. Your attitude toward them can score you a plum banquette by the window, or a wobbly table with a view of the bathrooms.

General managers (GMs) are the dons of the restaurant. They oversee the staff, solve problems, handle major complaints from diners, and generally make sure the restaurant is stocked, serving quality food, and running smoothly. Although they do most of their work behind the scenes, GMs often wander the dining room floor on busy nights. If you have good things to say about a meal or the staff, introduce yourself to the general manager and pay your compliments to the restaurant. If you're a regular or aspire to be one, this is how you'll get a GM (or maître d') to recognize you on the next visit.

LAGNIAPPE

GMs spend a lot of time with their staff, before and after hours. If you plan to lodge a serious complaint about the food or service, keep the exchange cordial and honest. Exaggerating your complaint or taking potshots at the staff will probably make the GM more sympathetic to the server's plight of dealing with a surly diner like you.

The **maître d'hôtel** (MAY-truh doh-TELL), or **maître d'** (may-truh DEE), is like the host of the party or the VIP concierge in a restaurant. If the restaurant is on fire, it's their job to make you think it's part of the entertainment. In addition to taking reservations, juggling seating arrangements, glad-handing guests, and acting as a liaison between the kitchen and the waitstaff, the main job of the maître d' is to cultivate relationships with customers and keep regulars happy. They also oversee front-of-the-house operations, like making sure table settings and other aesthetic details are up to snuff. Like GMs, maître d's are the people who handle problems, green-light freebies like appetizers, a glass of wine, or dessert, and can make you feel like an A-lister if they know your name. You want to know this person, and, more important, you want him or her to know you.

Sommeliers (saw-muh-LYAYS) are the wine gurus who put together the wine list, maintain the cellar, and help diners select wines to pair with their meal. Think of the sommelier as your personal wine country tour guide. Ask for it, and you'll get a mini-lecture on wine regions, grapes, dirt, weather, vintage, flavors, and aromas. Or, you can get straightforward pairing suggestions *sans* lecture. But first you have to tell your waiter, "I'd like to get some suggestions from the sommelier," then admit you don't know much about wine. Don't be afraid to say "I like Chardonnay" or "I usually drink Merlot because it's familiar" or even "I'm looking for a bottle in the $40 range." If you have a better grasp of wine styles, mention the basic characteristics of your favorite wines (red or white, name brands, grapes, etc.).

"It seems the higher up you go in dining, the more afraid people are to ask about wine. My favorite diners are the ones who say, 'I have no idea how to pick wine,' but they're willing to try new things and they're curious about why I selected a particular wine."

PATRICIA BORGARDT, sommelier,
Commander's Palace, New Orleans

Bartenders are the restaurant yentas: collectors and—if you play your cards right—disseminators of some of the most useful insider information in a restaurant. Show up twenty minutes before your reservation to have a drink at the bar, pay as soon as your drink arrives, and leave a generous cash tip. If the bar isn't slammed and you can strike up an easy conversation while you sip your drink, plumb bartenders for details about the best servers, the house specialties, menu favorites, and other miscellaneous tidbits about the food and the restaurant.

Want to be a bartender's friend? If your party has drinks at the bar before being seated, close the tab and tip the bartender separately (as opposed to carrying the tab over to your table). If you do transfer the tab, tip the bartender cash and remember to subtract those drinks from your final bill when figuring out how much to tip your waiter.

Waiters in upscale restaurants are often career professionals who love what they do, and do it well. The chances of getting a terrible waiter in fine dining are slim, but keep in mind that the service you get can also be a reflection of your attitude. It's best to think of the relationship as though you're sitting at the waiter's table, not *your* table. You're on their turf, and serving you is how they pay rent and buy groceries. They don't have to love you, but it helps if they like you. And it's not a one-way relationship: You're paying not just for the food, but for the service they're providing you. Feel free to float questions and ask for suggestions. Waiters see what goes in and out of the kitchen on a regular basis, so they know the chef's specialties, the portion sizes, the ingredients, the complaints, and the compliments people have about everything on the menu. Treat them with respect, use them for everything they know, and tip them well when they do their job well.

"As a waiter, you want to give the best service possible to please the customer and line your pockets. To do so, you need to understand the customer's expectations, and a good waiter can read a customer like a cop reads a perp. Then, you delve into the varying depths of your repertoire of serving skills to exceed those expectations."
ANDREW MORRISON, editor, Waiterblog.com

BACK-OF-THE-HOUSE STAFF

These are the people who touch your food. They may seem grumpy, uninterested, or unapproachable (you would be too after twelve hours on your feet in a roasting-hot kitchen), but if you get a chance to talk shop or throw compliments their way, do. Kitchen staff members are a rare and fascinating breed.

Executive chefs are the head honchos in the kitchen. They oversee the staff, food preparation, menu planning, and administrative details, like training, budget, and payroll. In celebrity chef restaurants, they are the celebrity chefs, or they may run several kitchens for a hotel or restaurant group.

Sous-chefs (SOO shehfs), literally "under the chef," are second in command in the kitchen. They cook, order supplies, supervise the kitchen staff, and are responsible for the day-to-day running of a kitchen.

Tournant chefs (toor-NAH shehfs) are the jacks-of-all-trades: They float from job to job in the kitchen, depending on where help is needed.

Station Chefs

Each morsel of food on your plate is prepared by a different chef who covers a specific station in the kitchen.

Chefs de partie are the lead chefs on any of the food stations.

Garde-mangers (gahrd mahn-ZHAYS) handle the cold food prep, including salads, dressings, appetizers, and sometimes desserts.

Rotisseurs (roh-TIHS-syurs), or grill or broiler chefs, are in charge of spit/oven-roasting, grilling, and frying meat, fish, poultry, game, and vegetables.

Sauciers (saw-SYAYS), or soup and sauce chefs, make stocks, sauces, soups, and garnishes.

Entremetiers (AHN-truh-meh-TYAYS), or vegetable chefs, prepare, cook, and plate all fruits, vegetables, cereals, grains, and beans.

Poissoniers (pwa-sohn-YAYS), or fish chefs, are responsible for cutting, preparing, and cooking fish.

Pâtissiers (pah-tees-SYAYS), or pastry chefs, create dessert menus and make all sweets and baked goods in the restaurant.

Money Talks: Tips and Bribes

Whatever your policy on tipping, whatever your feelings about greasing palms, remember that service has a price. If you want a better table or a shot at skipping the wait in a crowded restaurant, slipping cash into the right hand might make it happen. If you want extra attention while you're entertaining clients or anyone else you need to impress, patting a few bills into your waiter's hand will probably help. Officially, most restaurants will say that money doesn't buy better service or preferential treatment. Unofficially, it's standard practice to "take care" of the diners who "take care" of the staff. VIP treatment is normally reserved for rock stars and celebrities who bring dollars and cachet to a restaurant, or those generous regulars who frequent the place. But if you require a little extra TLC, anyone with a few bills and the tact to do it gracefully can pay to play.

How much grease does it take? "Front-end" tips depend on the restaurant, what you want, and how badly you want it. A $20 bill covers most scenarios, but the idea is to cough up enough to get the job done and appear to be generous. If you're prepared to spend $500 on a meal, an extra $40 to bypass the crowds or score a prime table might be worth it to you.

HOW TO PASS THE BUCK

Don't:

- hand off money if you can't pull it off like a pro.

- offer the general manager cash.

- slap a twenty on the host's stand or into a waiter's pocket.

- follow the cash with a list of demands.

- attempt a bribe if the restaurant is exclusive *and* packed—you're more likely to get snubbed.

Do:

- say "please" and "thank you." Fat tips don't give you license to act like spoiled royalty.

- tack on gracious phrases like "If there's anything you can do" or "We may need a little more of your time tonight" or "I see you're very busy" to your request.

- be discreet with the handoff. Fold the bill in half at least twice so that you can pass it in a handshake or slip it under a hand.

EAT THIS

The word *tip* is an English acronym for "to insure promptness."

HOW MUCH AND WHO: TIPS FOR TIPPING

The base wage a restaurant pays can be lower than $3 an hour. Imagine working an eight-hour shift on your feet hustling food and booze for a whopping $24 and you'll begin to understand why tips are a matter of survival for waiters and other restaurant staff. The basic range for tips is 10 to 20 percent, but tipping at the high end of the range is standard in ritzy restaurants.

Technically, tips are based on the pretax bill, but if the service is superb it probably won't kill you to fork out another buck or three for an after-tax-based tip, which is what most waiters expect. If you're in a large party, expect an automatic gratuity to be added to the final bill—usually 18 percent pretax for groups of six or more. Even if the gratuity has been added, you should top it off to 20 percent if the service was excellent.

Waiter: 15 to 20 percent

Bartender: 15 to 20 percent, or a minimum of $1 per drink

Sommelier: 10 to 15 percent of the wine tab

Coat check: $1 per coat if service is free; no tip if there's a fee

Parking valet: $2 per car

Powder room attendant: $1

Great tips aren't only about the Benjamins. If you're broke—or just too "frugal" to tip more than 10 percent—delivering a glowing review of your waiter to the general manager can compensate for a skimpy gratuity.

Bottle Service

Tipping the sommelier may seem excessive in a restaurant where waiters may be required to share their tips, but it's a nice gesture if he or she selected a great, reasonably priced bottle for your table. An extra 10 to 15 percent is generous for bottles under $100. If you choose a more expensive vintage, a flat $20 is standard.

TALES OF THE FEAST

Tipping was banned in six states—Washington, Mississippi, Arkansas, Tennessee, South Carolina, and Iowa—in the early 1900s. The punishment for the crime of soliciting or accepting a gratuity? A fine of $10 to $100, or up to thirty days of jail time.

Cash Is King

If you want to score points with a waiter or a bartender, leave cash tips even if you pay your bill with a credit card. Low on green? Split the tip between the credit card and cash. The IRS might not endorse this tactic, but it's a bonus for restaurant staff that can also bump you into "regular" status.

EAT THIS

A study conducted by the Center for Hospitality Research at the Cornell University School of Hotel Administration found that waiters in casual restaurants who squatted next to a table when they introduced themselves to customers increased tips by an average of 3 percent. (Note to self: squatting waiters = cheesy restaurant.)

From Nobody to VIP: How to Be a Regular

If there is one universal truth about the relationship between diners and restaurants, it is this: Regulars get the perks. Becoming a familiar face is how you reap the best benefits—the last-minute table on a Saturday night, the tip about the questionable halibut, the tasty experiments coming out of the kitchen. The beauty is, it doesn't take a trust fund or weekly visits to become a regular.

The Ten Commandments of a Regular

- Thou shalt leave cash tips, and occasionally overtip.

- Thou shalt know the names of and introduce thyself to bartenders, favorite waiters, the maître d'/host, and general manager.

- Thou shalt dine on Tuesday, Wednesday, or Sunday nights when the restaurant is usually dead.

- Thou shalt refer friends, family, clients, and coworkers who will tell the maître d'/host, "[Mere Mortal] loves this place and told me to check it out."

- Thou shalt dine at the restaurant on personal special occasions, but not major holidays (Christmas, New Year's) or Hallmark celebrations (Valentine's Day, Mother's Day) when amateurs and tourists fill the place and the staff is bitter about working.

- Thou shalt arrive early and go to the bar for a drink (even if it's nonalcoholic) before dinner.

- Thou shalt pay specific compliments about the waitstaff and food to the maître d' and general manager.

- Thou shalt dine there as often as financially possible; lunch, drinks, and solo meals at the bar count, too.

- Thou shalt take business colleagues to the restaurant as often as thy expense account allows.

- Thou shalt not presume elite status or expect special treatment, but graciously accept it when offered.

BE A BUFF

Tipping: An American Social History of Gratuities, by Kerry Segrave; *The Itty Bitty Guide to Tipping,* by Stacie Krajchir and Carrie Rosten; *Fodor's FYI: How to Tip; Tipping for Success: Secrets for How to Get In and Get Great Service,* by Mark L. Brenner

2

WHEREFORK ART THOU?

the ART of EATING and BEHAVING at the TABLE

Here's the deal: Reaching for the wrong wineglass or inadvertently swiping your dinner companion's roll won't get you tossed from any restaurant. But when you're surrounded by seventeen pieces of fine tableware and trying to act sophisticated, realizing you're the only one without a napkin in your lap or that you've used your neighbor's bread plate is just the kind of thing you want to avoid at a business dinner or a formal luncheon with the future in-laws. Feeling comfortable and capable in a ritzy restaurant is all about getting back to the basics: learning the boundaries of your place-setting turf, knowing how to use all those shiny forks, and understanding the rudimentary rules of table etiquette.

Your Turf on a Formal Table: Navigating a Proper Place Setting

Forget about memorizing the shapes and sizes of the different utensils, plates, and glasses. Follow one simple rule of thumb: Start with the outside flatware, set farthest away from your plate, and with each new course use the next utensil in the setting, moving inside toward your plate. Yes, there may be a spoon on the far right and a fork on the far left, but only one of those utensils is for the soup course. Familiarize yourself with this classic table setting, and you should have no problems finding your way through the flatware maze. You will no doubt run into slight variations of this setting, but if you follow the "outside to inside" rule, you can't go wrong. Also, servers at high-end restaurants typically set, remove, and replace tableware as it's needed, which takes even more guesswork out of the equation.

*"The most important thing to remember in fine dining
is to relax and don't take it too seriously. If you don't
know which fork to use or how to pronounce a word or the
correct way to eat something, have a laugh about it.
I guarantee in most cases the waiter will laugh with you
and say, 'I'm with you. I don't get it, either.'"*
—RICK BAYLESS, chef/owner, Topolobampo, Chicago

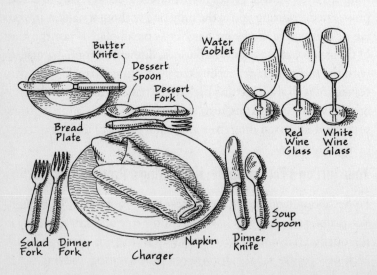

Your **napkin** may be laid in the middle of your plate, stuffed into your water glass, or set to the left of your fork setting. As soon as everyone at your table is seated, unfold the napkin and lay it across your lap. (A waiter may do this for you.) When you leave the table, whether it's the middle of the meal or the end, loosely gather the napkin and set it to the left of your plate; don't leave it on the seat of your chair.

TALES OF THE FEAST

In first-century A.D. Rome, dinner guests brought their own sizable napkins, called *mappa*, to parties and toted leftovers home in them. During the Renaissance period, men laid a napkin over their left shoulder and used it to clean utensils and cups throughout the meal. An old European superstition holds that guests who lay a napkin in their chair will never eat at that table again. (It's also a practical custom: Food tidbits and schmears stay on napkins—and off your rear.)

Think of the **charger** or **service plate**—the large plate underneath the dinner plate or napkin—as a purely aesthetic dish that keeps spills off the tablecloth. It is not a big bread plate. Do not eat off of it. In traditional fine dining, your waiter carries the plate away with the dishes from your first course. Or, plates and bowls for each course are set on top of the charger, and it is removed at the end of the meal, before dessert.

Your **bread plate**, the small dish at ten o'clock above the charger, may or may not have a small butter knife laid across it. If no butter knife is set, use the "master" knife that is passed with the butter or your clean dinner knife.

Many people commit the most basic fine dining crime when they try to eat bread. *Do not bite into a whole roll or slice of bread.* Take a whole piece of bread from the basket, place it on your plate, then tear off bite-sized chunks to butter and eat. If olive oil is passed, drizzle a tablespoon or two on your bread plate—don't turn your plate into a wading pool. At seriously formal meals, you may not have a bread plate, in which case you should rest your bread on the edge of your dinner plate.

In France, if bread plates aren't set, diners place their bread directly on the table where this plate would be. The French also invented the *ramasse miettes,* or "crumb collector," the long metal scraper waiters use to sweep specks of food from the table. Coincidence? *Au contraire.*

TALES OF THE FEAST

The practice of keeping your lips off of whole pieces of bread dates to medieval times, when leftovers were handed down to diners at lower tables. Tearing off pieces instead of biting directly into bread was a practical way to make the trickle-down buffet more hygienic.

The **salad fork**, the outermost utensil to the left of your plate, may have a thicker left tine and is smaller than a dinner fork. If you're dining in a true French restaurant, the salad fork is set closest to your plate because the salad course is served after the entrée.

You can hold your **dinner fork**, situated immediately left of the plate, two ways: American-style, tines-up in your dominant hand and anchored between your middle finger and thumb, or European-style, tines-down in your left hand with your index finger extended along the back. Rest your utensils tines-up, blade-in vertically on the sides of your plate when you are not using them. The handles should not touch the table again once you have used your flatware.

A **fish fork** is typically delivered before the fish course, and is smaller than the dinner fork. Before stainless steel was introduced in the 1920s, when most utensils were made of steel, fish forks were traditionally made of sterling silver, which does not react with lemon or other acidic sauces often served with fish.

The **salad knife** is the outermost knife in the setting.

The **dinner knife**, placed directly to the right of the plate, is used for the salad and fish course if additional knives are not set. To use a knife the American way: Pin food with the fork tine-down in your nondominant hand and cut with the knife in the dominant hand, lay the knife across the top edge of the plate, then switch the fork back to the dominant hand to spear and eat the morsel. The Euro way: Cut and corral food onto the fork using the knife in the dominant hand, keeping the fork in the nondominant hand to deliver the bite. After using your knife, lay it blade-in across the top right edge of your plate.

A **steak knife** is usually delivered with the meat course.

A **teaspoon** is placed during coffee service, or sits between the knife and soupspoon.

A **soupspoon** is the outermost utensil to the right of the plate. The bowl of a spoon should not pass through your lips in a restaurant. You can slurp soup out of the can at home, but in public, dip your soupspoon away from your body, scoop three-quarters of a spoonful, then bring the edge of the spoon to your lips, tilt the bowl slightly, and sip.

Dessert flatware is usually placed at the top of the plate with the bowl of the spoon pointing left and fork tines to the right, or it may be set with the dessert course.

LAGNIAPPE

When in doubt about any table manner matter, glance around the table or dining room and copy your host or the classiest act in the place.

There's absolutely no risk of grabbing your neighbor's glassware in a formal table setting—a grouping that can contain up to five different vessels—if you can remember that your glasses are always on the right side of your plate. Your waiter will fill each glass with the appropriate liquid and remove and set glasses as needed, depending on what you order to sip.

Should your life depend on selecting the right glassware in a blindfold test, this will save your skin: The **water goblet** is laid at one o'clock above the dinner knife and is the glass farthest left in the grouping. In über-traditional, multicourse place settings, a small **sherry** or **aperitif glass** may be set above and to the right of the water glass. Your **red wineglass**, which typically has a more bulbous bowl, sits to the right of the water glass. The **white wineglass** has a narrower bowl and may be set slightly below, but always to the right of the red wineglass. A **champagne flute**, if one is set, is placed above and between the red and white wineglasses.

TALES OF THE FEAST

Restaurants serve meals *à la russe* (Russian-style): Each course is plated and served individually. To serve *à la française,* or what we think of as family-style, many dishes are set on the table or served at once. A Russian ambassador introduced plated service to Paris in 1810, but Auguste Escoffier, the granddaddy of luxury French dining, is widely credited with popularizing the style after incorporating it at the Savoy Hotel and Carlton Hotel in London.

Keep Your Elbows Off the Table: A Refresher on Acting Polite and Polished

Basic manners are something you should know by the time you're allowed to sit at the grown-up table, but it's easy to forget some of the finer points of dining etiquette when you eat most of your meals out of Styrofoam boxes. These table tips are simply gentle reminders of what you probably already know, but may need to brush up on.

- Don't order the most expensive wine or entrée on the menu unless the credit card is coming out of your wallet.

- Wait until everyone at your table is served before you dig in, unless the host or guest of honor insists that you start eating.

- Always pass the salt and pepper together, even if a tablemate asks for only one of them, so dinner guests won't have to search for orphaned shakers.

- Don't salt, pepper, or otherwise condiment-ize your food before you taste it.

- Don't blow on your food to cool it off. If it's too hot to eat, take the hint. Wait.

- Whenever a woman leaves the table or returns to sit, all men seated with her should stand up.

- Keep your elbows—and car keys, lip balm, sunglasses, purse, iPod, Blackberry, and so on—off the table. Your personal doodads are not only aesthetically out of place, they also create an obstacle course your waiter must maneuver around.

- Licking a utensil, even if it's covered in buttery, creamy goodness, is rude. Deftly mopping sauces, soup, and tasty giblets with a piece of bread, however, is *French*. This may be taboo in front of VIPs, but if devouring every last dribble of food is your focus—not making a sterling impression on fellow diners—it's okay to make a clean sweep of the good stuff with bread.

- Mind your peas and couscous. Use a piece of bread or your knife to corral hard-to-stab or -scoop items onto your fork instead of chasing them around your plate.

- The light clatter of tableware in a restaurant is normal, but try to minimize clanging and scraping metal utensils against dishes (think: nails on a chalkboard). Gently stir liquids, like coffee, without banging the spoon inside the cup or tapping the spoon on the rim. Slice, don't saw, with your knife. Ladle, don't dredge, with your soupspoon.

- Set any passed item, whether it's the salt and pepper shakers, a bread basket, or a butter plate, directly on the table instead of passing hand-to-hand.

- Never intercept a pass. Snagging a roll out of the breadbasket or taking a shake of salt when it's en route to someone else is technically a no-no.

- Take small bites. Noshing on a fist-sized hunk of meat will make it difficult to engage in dinner chitchat in a timely or graceful way. By the same token, avoid asking questions of other diners who are trying to masticate.

- Do not pick up food off the floor, even if you're the reason it ended up there. The staff is trained to deal with spills and accidental food launchings, but if the mishap goes unnoticed, simply call it to your waiter's attention.

- Always position your knife so that the sharp side of the blade is in, facing you.

TALES OF THE FEAST

Keeping the business side of your knife aimed inward conveys a lack of ill will or intention toward other diners, which wasn't always the case at ancient banquets. A tragic combination of plentiful food, booze, and talk of politics in close proximity to handy table weaponry occasionally led to bloodshed at the table.

- Do not push your dishes away or stack them for the waiter when you are finished eating. Leave plates and glasses where they are set.

- Do not groom yourself at the table. Using a toothpick, reapplying lipstick, powdering or blowing your nose, attempting to remove a stain on your tie, and fiddling with your contacts are all done behind closed bathroom doors, not in front of other diners.

- Once used, your utensils, including the handles, should not touch the table again. Always rest forks, knives, and spoons on the side of your plate or in a bowl.

Millennium Manners:
Civilized Solutions for Modern Faux Pas

Today, chucking your ungnawed bread to the next table or stabbing a fellow diner would qualify as more than just "bad manners," yet many seemingly obsolete guidelines for acting civilized at the table remain intact, like keeping your mouth off of bread or facing your knife blade inward. So it stands to reason that there are some modern-day no-nos and restaurant scenarios we face with no clue of how to handle ourselves because there is no precedent or tradition. Fear not with these contemporary dining dos and don'ts.

Cancellations and no-shows: Never flake out of a reservation without calling to cancel. Some restaurants take credit card numbers to hold reservations and charge no-show fees without at least twenty-four hours' notice of the cancellation. But failing to cancel will do more than put a dent in your wallet. Like parking in a handicap space or unloading twenty-seven items in the express checkout, it's bad restaurant juju that will come back to haunt you.

Screaming babies and wandering kids: Do not confront junior's parents on your own. A well-trained restaurant staff should address any pint-sized problems. Politely explain the disturbance to your waiter and ask "Is it possible for us to move to a different table?" or "Would you mind talking to the parents?"

Celebrity sightings: Do not feed, approach, pet, photograph, ask for an autograph, follow to the restroom, or wave "howdy" to a VIP in a restaurant, no matter how big a fan you are. Restaurants are private territory. Fawning, gawking fans are to celebrities what those rose-peddling, Polaroid-taking entrepreneurs who sneak through restaurants are to you: annoying and tacky.

Obvious snubs: If the host seats table after table ahead of you while you wait—and *wait*—for your reservation to be honored, or the service is terrible (think: empty water glasses, snarky waiters, endless waits for food, and no apologies), you have two options: (1) leave the restaurant and vow never to return or (2) wait it out and hope the management makes up for it in complimentary food or drinks. In either case, don't be a doormat. You have an obligation to speak up for yourself and put the restaurant on notice.

How to Handle Bad Service

If you get jerked around by a host or a waiter, mimic his or her moves when you confront them. Adjust your body language and tone of voice to match, whether they play it nicey-nice or icy and condescending. Blatant snubbers expect people to react or retreat. But copying their behavior—using the same hand gestures and volume, repeating the excuses they give you before you slip in your point, holding eye contact—is a psychological switcheroo. They're more likely to give you what you want if you play on the same level without escalating or deflating the situation.

Chitchat overload: Both waiters and diners are guilty of turning what should be a brief exchange into a blathering personal monologue. You can handle waiters who volunteer too much information—about personal issues, the fascinating journey of tonight's asparagus, the weather—or who repeatedly interrupt your dinner conversation with a friendly brush-off: "Thanks for the attention. You've been great. I think we're all set with the order, right?" By the same token, don't monopolize your server's time with your own meanderings about the first time you ate escargots or your wine-tasting trip to Napa. It's polite to ask "How is your night going?" to find out if your waiter is slammed, and you should gauge your interaction based on the answer. Even if your waiter is in the weeds, he or she is obliged to listen to everything you have to say, so keep the friendly small talk and dithering over what to order—while your waiter patiently *waits*—to a minimum.

Rowdy cohorts: If you know you will be dining with someone who is loud, hard of hearing, or prone to sloppy, drunken scenes or fits of glass-shattering laughter, do everyone a favor: Ask for a private room or a sound-muffling corner in the restaurant when you make a reservation. As the host of a gathering, it's your responsibility to keep your guests in line, but prior warning can help the host accommodate you and keep any VIPs or regulars out of range.

SOCIAL DISGRACES

It's natural to let your guard down when you're dining with family or friends because they'll forgive and forget your table transgressions. But when you're on an all-out mission to impress fellow diners, whether they include business contacts or the future Mr. or Mrs., these tips can keep you out of trouble.

Order clean. Don't even think about the whole lobster, mussels in white wine sauce, angel hair pasta, gooey short ribs, grilled asparagus, or the frisee salad. Bypass any food that requires a bib, wet wipes, your fingers, utensils you're not com-

fortable using, or a concerted effort to fork, peel, or cut gracefully. Stick with steak, chicken, and boneless, skinless fish—
foods that are easy to manage with a fork and knife.

Say no to "to go." Your last impression is as important as
your first. If you trot off into the sunset with your leftovers
wrapped in a foil swan or at the bottom of a giant shopping
bag, here's the lasting image you're leaving behind: you, standing in front of the refrigerator in your skivvies at 4 A.M. eating
those cold leftovers directly out of the container. Not pretty.

Never order a Long Island iced tea. Ever. Or a white Russian, a sea breeze, a screwdriver, or any other drink native to
college bars and fraternity basements. If you drink, order
wine or classic cocktails only.

Stifle your fussy eating habits. Keep those "on the side" and
"fat-free" requests to a minimum, and don't ask to have the
food preparation, side dishes, or sauces changed from what's
offered on the menu. Order around your allergies and health
concerns without explanation. This is not the time to discuss
the Atkins diet or your fear of orange foods, or to demonstrate just how picky, fragile, or high maintenance you can be.

DEAD RINGER

One contemporary faux pas deserves a category all its own: cell
phones. If you want to be a class act, follow these simple rules.

Turn off your cell phone or set it on vibrate. Whether it's
Beethoven's Fifth or Limp Bizkit's "Nookie," your ring tone
is not what the restaurant had in mind for creating ambience.

Do not dial or answer calls at the table—*ever.* No matter
how discreet or soft-spoken you think you are, it's unforgiv-
ably rude to the people you're dining with, not to mention

the nearby diners who definitely do not want to hear about your after-dinner plans or brutal day at work.

If you absolutely must make or take a call, excuse yourself from the table. But you'd better have a very good excuse. Either fake a trip to the bathroom or apologize with a sincerely worthy reason, such as "The hospital just called. I think they might've found my kidney match."

Step outside, even if it's hailing or below zero. The common areas in a restaurant—the bathroom, the bar, and the waiting area by the host's stand—are not your private phone booth. If anyone is inconvenienced by the call, it should be you.

Make it quick. Keep the conversation under five minutes and apologize again to your dining companions when you return.

Dinner Diplomacy: From Funky Food to "Finished!"

UNSWALLOWABLE FOOD OBJECTS (UFOS)

Funky bites happen. When it is feasible, bones, pits, shells, and other UFOs should be removed from your mouth the same way they entered. If a bite with bone in it or an olive with a pit is delivered by fork, discreetly expel the tidbit back onto your fork and deposit it on the side of your plate (preferably under a piece of bread). If an olive gained entry by way of fingers, the pit can be removed with your fingers. But if unloading an inedible scrap onto your fork will create more of a spectacle, pinch the item between your thumb and forefinger and swiftly remove it.

"Grin and swallow" is the basic rule for other unsavory bites, but if you chomp into something you can't possibly bear to swallow—gristle, a fish eyeball, something suspiciously gritty, crunchy, or gelatinous—keep a straight face, bring your napkin to your mouth, discreetly release the food into one corner as if wiping your mouth, and roll it up. Then ask your waiter to bring you a fresh napkin.

HOW TO SIGNAL "FINISHED" TO A WAITER

From course to course your tableware will be whisked away and replaced as needed, and you shouldn't try to help out or attempt to signal "Bring on the next course!" by stacking your plates, bowls, and utensils for the waiter. To have your place setting cleared (and avoid any confusion over whether you're saving that corner of fillet for the last bite), rest your fork tines-up and knife blade-in with the handles resting at five o'clock and tips pointing to ten o'clock on your plate. If you're taking a break from eating, but fully intend to make a last sweep of that béarnaise sauce, lay your utensils vertically on either side of your plate. Between cuts, rest your knife across the top edge of the plate.

BE A BUFF

The Art of the Table, by Suzanne von Drachenfels; *The Bulfinch Anatomy of Antique China and Silver,* by Tim Forrest; *Feast: A History of Grand Eating,* by Roy Strong; *The Rituals of Dinner: The Origins, Evolution, Eccentricities and Meaning of Table Manners,* by Margaret Visser

3

FOLLOWING ORDERS

from **MENU SPECIALS** *to small* **PLATES,**

how to **GET** *what you* **WANT**

So, you've made it to the table without tripping in your fancy shoes. Congratulations! Your next challenge: *la carte*. That's French for "the menu"—your first lesson in translating and understanding those encyclopedias of tastiness you're handed at the beginning of a meal. To be sure, the descriptions in a hefty, leather-bound menu can be pure poetry, with each extravagant ingredient or culinary twist evoking anticipation and awe. At the same time, menus can stoke a lot of the anxieties we have about fine dining, namely that we're paying a premium for something we don't completely understand. Table manners and restaurant etiquette are important, but to feel truly at ease in these culinary utopias and further your fine dining education, you have to know how to read a menu and order from the many different types of menus you may run into.

Menu Voodoo: Understanding Restaurant Tricks, Chef's Tastings, and Small Plates

You know that sinking feeling you get when a menu thuds as it hits the table and you see pages—*pages*—of different courses to thumb through? If you're not an adventurous eater to begin with, a gigantic menu can confirm all of those fears you have about food you can't pronounce. Even if you're a foodie, the volume of information you need to absorb to be able to order the perfect meal can be daunting. Worrying about how many "small plates" to order or fussing over the details of what's in a chef's tasting can knock the wind out of a high-flying meal, to the point that you end up ordering safe—the roasted chicken or the steak—instead of venturing into the great and tasty unknown. Buckle up, Mere Mortal. Intimidating menus are about to get a whole lot easier.

TRICKS OF THE TRADE

Restaurants are not above using psychology to steer you into ordering higher-profit dishes. Not all restaurants do this, and chain restaurants are guilty of the more tacky and obvious ploys, like boxing items or throwing fireworks all over a menu to dazzle you into ordering the $12.95 prime rib. High-end restaurants employ more subtle devices, like putting popular and higher-profit dishes in the first or last spot on a list because diners read those descriptions more thoroughly and order those dishes more often. A diner's eye tends to gravitate toward the top right-hand side of the menu, and lingers on the middle of three pages, so restaurants place signature or profitable dishes accordingly. They also tuck the price of a dish at the end of its description and may omit the dollar sign, as if to say, "Let's not sully this experience with the crass talk of money."

Restaurants are, first and foremost, businesses that must be profitable to stay afloat. As long as you know the menu tricks going in, there's no reason to feel like the restaurant is trying to dupe you. This is also why it's important to ask questions and spend as much time as you need looking over a menu. No two restaurants are alike, but the more you study a variety of menus, the better you'll be at spotting the good stuff, staying away from the amateur dishes, and knowing when something is a good deal. The best restaurants, like all the others, want to make money, but they also want you to walk away feeling like it was money well spent. One menu trick in your favor: look for "loss leaders"—marquee dishes designed to impress diners with expensive, rare ingredients like black truffles and Kobe beef. Often, these pricey dishes cost more to make than the restaurant charges for them. But it's probably bad karma to order a dish solely because you think the restaurant will lose money on it.

FULL-COURSE MENUS

Classic French meals start with hot or cold **hors d'oeuvres**, such as charcuterie (cured meat), escargots (snails in butter), galette (filled pastry tart), or pâté. The **entrée**, not to be confused with the American variety, is a starter course of soup, like consommé (clear) or a potage (creamy), or sometimes an egg-based dish like quiche or a savory soufflé. Although it's less common now, at very formal dinners back in the day, the **poisson** (fish) course was served before **la plat**, the main meat course. Now, it's usually one or the other—a classic meaty dish like coq au vin, boeuf bourguignonne, or cassoulet, or a fish-based course, like sole meunière or saumon en papillote. In France and in many French restaurants, the salad course follows the main course. Finally, **le fromage** (cheese) course is served, followed by—or instead of—**les entremets** (dessert or sweets).

Classic Italian meals start with the **antipasti** ("before meal")—hot or cold appetizers like prosciutto di Parma and melon; insalata caprese, a salad of buffalo mozzarella, tomatoes, and basil; bruschetta (broo-SKET-ah); or crostini (krohs-TEE-nee), toasted bread slices rubbed with garlic and olive oil and topped with cheese, fresh tomato, seafood or meat, fried calamari, or mixed grilled vegetables. The **primi**, or first course, is traditionally a dish served in a bowl, like soup, risotto, polenta, or pasta in broth or sauce. It is customary to order the **secondi** (main course) of meat, chicken, or fish and **contorni** (vegetable side dishes) after the first course. This gives you a chance to decide how hungry you are and order accordingly. Typical dishes include osso buco (braised lamb shank), veal piccata (veal sautéed in butter and lemon), and saltimbocca (wine-sautéed veal with prosciutto and sage). **Formaggi**, cheese courses, are slowly becoming more popular, but aren't as common. The meal ends with **dulci**, the dessert course.

TASTING AND CHEF'S MENUS

When you want to experience an all-out food bonanza that showcases a chef's best work, order a tasting menu, or *menu dégustation* (deh-guh-STAYshn). These multicourse meals are the chef's selection of specially prepared dishes that are not on the regular menu. Tastings have a set number of courses, but many restaurants give you the option of having a small, medium, or large tasting—say, five, ten, or fifteen courses. Once you order and tell your waiter about any food issues, the chef does the rest.

Ideally, a tasting menu shows off seasonal or local ingredients and features a balance of flavors, textures, and temperatures that play off of each other and aren't overwhelming to the palate or monotonous over the long haul. In high-caliber restaurants, tasting menus offer you a chance to sample a chef's specialties and venture into unfamiliar terrain without too much of a commitment. The courses tend to be more complex to prepare and feature unusual, luxury ingredients, but they're also small.

DO Order a Tasting Menu:

- on a weeknight or Saturday afternoon, when you have time for a three- to four-hour meal.

- to experience a chef's true talents.

- if you're unfamiliar with the cuisine but want to try new things.

- if you're a regular, and you know the chef will set you up with the best.

- when the focus will be on the food, not business.

DON'T Order a Tasting Menu:

- if you're in a hurry. These meals unfold at a leisurely pace, and you probably won't want to hit the dance floor after a full tasting.

- for one if you're a table of four. Restaurants require the entire party to join in to keep the timing of the courses in sync.

- during business dinners, unless someone at the table insists. The onslaught of courses will distract.

- on Sunday. Chances are, you're getting older or leftover bits and pieces.

SMALL PLATES, MAMMOTH MENUS

You know you're in for it if the waiter says, "Let me explain the way the menu works." Taking a cue from the Spanish tapas trend, some restaurants are exploiting our love of little plates with monolithic menus featuring a zillion categories of small, appetizer-like dishes. The upside is that you have the freedom to build your own tasting and the variety is a nice change of pace from the soup-salad-entrée routine. The downside: Thumbing through eight pages of tidbits can be more overwhelming than fun. Take these hints for narrowing your options.

- **Set limits.** Little plates can add up to big tabs. Keep a mental tally and spend what you'd pay for a comparable meal.

- **Size up the dish.** Ask your waiter, "How many grilled sardines are in an order?" or "How big is the mushroom puff pastry?"

- **Think balance.** Order dishes from different food groups (veggie, meat, starch, dairy) with flavors and textures that complement and contrast each other.

- **Don't be bullied.** The waiter may explain how "most people" order, but there are no rules with this nontraditional menu.

- **Aim low.** Start with two or three plates per person. You can always order more.

Get a Culinary Clue: Speaking the Language of Fine Food

DEALS ON MEALS

The all-you-can-eat country buffet may be the last bastion of straightforward menu pricing. Things get trickier in swanky restaurants, but don't let the wording and abbreviations stump you.

À la carte items are priced individually on the menu. In a classic steakhouse, if you order steak à la carte, you'll pay more for additional side dishes, like a baked potato and creamed spinach, to go with it.

A.Q. is short for "as quoted" by the waiter, and generally means the same thing as **M.P.** (market price). It is used for specials and tasting menus with prices that fluctuate according to season and availability.

Prix fixe (PREE FIHKS) or "fixed price" dinners are multicourse meals with a preset price. Some restaurants offer choices for each course, some don't. **Table d'hôte** (table of the host) is also a multicourse meal, but it is served for the price listed with the entrée.

HOW'S THAT COOKED?

Admit it: You nod and smile and pretend to understand the waiter as he rattles on about pan-seared this and braised that from the list of specials. Nod with confidence the next time around by knowing these typical cooking techniques.

Bake: to cook in an oven using dry heat.

Barbecue: to slow-cook meat in a covered pit or on a grill heated by coals or wood.

Blacken: to rub meat or fish in a blend of spices and quickly cook it in a lightly oiled red-hot cast-iron skillet, which creates a crispy crust around the food.

Blanch: to dunk food, usually vegetables, into boiling water for a certain amount of time—anywhere from a few seconds to several minutes—then into ice-cold water to stop cooking.

Braise: to brown meat in fat over high heat, then slow-cook it, tightly covered, in a small amount of liquid for a long time. Vegetables may also be braised in hot liquids, such as chicken stock.

Brine: to marinate food in a strong salt-water or sugar-water solution, usually for pickling and preserving. Brining also makes meat, fish, or seafood more juicy and plump.

Broil: to cook directly under or over a heat source, such as a charcoal fire or a gas flame.

Butterfly: to slice food down the center, but not completely in half, so that it is "hinged" in the middle and can be splayed open.

Grill: to cook food on a grate set over hot coals or another high-heat source.

Infuse: to extract flavor from an herb, a spice, a fruit, or a vegetable by steeping it in a hot liquid or sauce. Tea, for example, is an infusion.

Pan-broil: a method of cooking meat or fish quickly in a heavy, unoiled pan over high heat.

Plank: to bake, broil, or grill meat or fish on a wooden board made of cedar, mesquite, hickory, or oak to impart a smoky flavor.

Poach: to cook food at a low simmer, or just below a boil, in a liquid such as broth, salted water, or wine.

Reduce: to boil a liquid such as stock or wine until most of the water evaporates and a thicker, more concentrated liquid or glaze is left.

Roast: to cook uncovered in an oven.

Sauté: to cook with a little oil or butter in a skillet over direct heat.

Sear: to brown meat quickly in a very hot skillet, broiler, or oven to seal in the juices; further cooking at a lower heat may be required on thicker cuts.

Simmer: to cook food in liquid heated to just below a boil.

Steep: to soak in a hot liquid.

Stew: to cook by covering food in liquid and simmering, covered, for a long time.

Order Up: Waiter-Diner Dialogue

You're seated at the table, napkin in lap, menu in hand, and your waiter is at the ready. What's next? Here's a walk-through of what to say and do when it's time to place your order.

SCENE 1: APERITIFS

The waiter asks, "Would you like something to drink?" It's a simple question, yet your inner-spaz is sputtering, "Uhhh, I haven't made it through the wine list. I don't know what I want for dinner. *What the hell do I say?*" No need to panic. Don't get rushed into ordering a bottle of wine if you're undecided. Tell your waiter, "I still need a little time with the menu and wine list to decide," then say:

"Water is fine for now."

"I'll take a bottle of sparkling water."

"I'll have a (insert your favorite aperitif) in the meantime."

"I'd like to chat with the sommelier first."

SCENE 2: SPECIALS

The waiter recites a long list of specials, but the dishes he describes all run together in your mind. Instead of trying to grasp every detail about a special, focus on the centerpiece of each dish. This will help you parse what you may be in the mood for and what's a definite "no" on your list. Even if all you can remember is "tongue," "filet mignon," and "lobster," you can ask the server to repeat certain specials instead of going over the entire list again.

Also ask your waiter, "Which dish exemplifies this restaurant?" Servers might push the crowd-pleaser (which they'll describe by saying "Everybody orders . . ." or "Lots of people like . . ."), but home in on the strange specialty dishes introduced by "This isn't popular, but the staff loves . . ." or "The chef is known for . . ."

Ordering is also the discovery phase of the meal. Now is the time to find out how dishes are prepared, learn what miscellaneous or mysterious ingredients they contain, and discuss any allergies, dietary quirks, or food phobias. Unless you're asking if the kitchen can remove all of the calories from your lamb or cook to your very rigid lacto-ovo-vegetarian, parsley-phobic specifications, a good waiter wants to know all of these details up front so he can steer you away from dishes you won't like (which also have a funny way of affecting his tip). It's also in the waiter's best interest to make sure you don't go into anaphylactic shock in the middle of the restaurant because you didn't realize there were peanuts in a dish. If you have any allergies or aversions, ask for recommendations that suit your tastes and special needs without divulging all of the gory details about what will happen if you eat cucumbers or shellfish. Focus more on what you like instead of harping on all of your dislikes.

What Waiters Want You to Ask

- "Is the soup cream-based?"

- "What, exactly, is *confit*?"

- "I need to stay away from cucumber, but I love light, herby sauces and pork. Do you recommend anything?"

- "Will you repeat the fish special?"

- "I'm on a reduced-salt diet. Can we cut some of the salt out of this dish without too much trouble?"

- "I'm vegetarian. Does the asparagus soup have a meat-based stock?"

- "How big is the pork chop?"

- "Can I get that with no sauce, or sauce on the side?"

- "Can you make sure that none of the food touches any other food on my plate?" (Just kidding.)

SCENE 3: THE MAIN EVENT

Once you're ready to order, keep it simple. List the dishes you want in the order you want to receive them, along with any additional instructions about how you want the food to be prepared. With steaks and other meat dishes that are cooked to order, it's helpful to throw in your definition of what rare, medium, or well-done means. If medium is "no pink in the middle" to you, the waiter needs to be able to convey that to the kitchen.

A WORD FOR THE PICKY EATERS

You probably know who you are, but here's a hint: "Can I have the petit filet, but instead of mushrooms, can I have it with béarnaise sauce? And I don't like asparagus. You have green beans in tonight's special, so can I have those instead? Would it be too much trouble to get those steamed, not roasted, and without thyme butter?" Sound familiar?

Here's the deal: unless there are allergies, serious phobias, or health issues involved, don't ask to have the basic preparation of a dish changed or request a swap of sauces or ingredients for something you like more or believe will go better with a dish. Yes, this is a "service industry," and most restaurants will try to accommodate any reasonable request (as well as some of the ridiculous ones). But consider the fallout of frivolous menu tinkering: The kitchen staff in high-end restaurants are able to turn out consistently stellar food because they've perfected most dishes to a routine science. They have a smooth system for creating those culinary masterpieces, and nitpicky requests can throw the system off-kilter. It's not a crime to ask for polenta instead of mashed potatoes if both are on the menu, or to get the sauce "on the side," but if it's not crucial, let it go. Don't forget that one of the reasons you're paying big bucks to eat in a fancy restaurant is to have a special experience. Like an artist's canvas, the food on your plate is the chef's masterpiece. Every ingredient and culinary twist that goes into making your food is designed by the chef to produce a singular, extraordinary experience for you, the diner. Half the thrill of eating at a chichi restaurant is trying new things, so leave it to the professionals. The chef knows best.

WAITER, I DIDN'T ORDER THIS

Your server may bring you an exquisite little morsel of food, like a bite-sized puff pastry filled with some mysterious yum or a demitasse (think: really small cup) of dreamy liquid. This surprise tidbit, called an *amuse bouche* (ah-mewz BOOSH), or mouth amusement, comes compliments of the chef—a delicious gift to tickle your taste buds and welcome you to the restaurant. In France and most of Europe it is called an *amuse gueule* (GEURL), or "palate amusement."

Dessert: Hitting Your Sweet Spot

Oh, you shouldn't. You couldn't possibly. After gorging on all of those rich, savory courses, who could even think of ordering dessert? Yeah, right. Even if you think you can't eat another bite, you should know how to spot the truly outstanding desserts—the ones that are worth blowing more dough and those Weight Watchers points on—and why you want to avoid particular pastries and sweets, depending on the season.

PRAISE THE PÂTISSIER

Although some restaurants get by with frozen sweets and pastry and others outsource their dessert menus to local bakeries (which isn't necessarily a bad thing), many great restaurants employ a pastry chef whose sole purpose in life is to create those flaming, oozing, flaky, creamy confections that can make the hours on a treadmill seem oh so worth it. Seeing the work of an in-house pastry chef shows how much thought a restaurant is putting into what it offers. You can always ask your waiter if the pastry chef makes all of the desserts, or clue in to these telltale signs:

- the pastry chef's name on the dessert menu

- individually baked portions, like mini-tarts or cakes, instead of slices

- bonus baked treats, like petits fours, that come with your coffee

"I stay away from overly constructed desserts. If it has a million frilly things, like caramel threads, rice noodles, and pyramids of chocolate all stacked into a tower or served in an edible box, it looks great but the flavor isn't striking. Anything with more than three primary ingredients is probably too much."
—SUSAN LIFRIERI, director of culinary administration, French Culinary Institute

DESSERT MENU BASICS

Sweets in swanky restaurants fall into three categories: classics, specialties, and seasonal. Most restaurants will offer a little bit of something from each category.

The **classics** are those rich treats you always see on dessert menus, like crème brûlée, molten chocolate cake, tiramisu, and cheesecake. Because these are the most popular and familiar desserts, they're usually the most consistent. Classics are good if you want something you're guaranteed to like—because you've had it a million times before—but it probably means dessert won't be as inventive or exciting.

The **specialties** are also always on the menu. They're designed to impress you, but also to carry through the theme of the restaurant, like all-organic, fusion, or ethnic. Specialty desserts tend to involve more bizarre ingredients or elaborate presentations, but these innovative creations stand out from the rest and offer you something totally different from the classics.

Seasonal desserts are usually fruit-based and rotate on and off the menu according to availability. You'll see pies or crisps with berries or stone fruits, ice cream, and sorbets in the summer; apple, pear, and citrus crisps and tarts in the winter. These desserts don't stay on a menu for very long, so they may not be as consistent, but they'll be the most fresh. Stay away from out-of-season desserts, like apple pies in the summer or berry crisps in the winter. Unless the restaurant has its own year-round greenhouse, off-season fruit is a sign they're serving frozen goods.

BE A BUFF

Food Lover's Companion, by Sharon Tyler Herbst; *A Meal Observed*, by Andrew Todhunter; *Near a Thousand Tables: A History of Food*, by Felipe Fernandez-Armesto; *Food in History*, by Reay Tannahill; *Feast: A History of Grand Eating*, by Roy Strong

4

BOOZE CLUES

DRINKING *to* **ENHANCE** *a* **MEAL—***not* **DROWN** *it*

Along with great company, good food only gets better with good drink. Whether it's a light aperitif to stoke your appetite and put you in the right frame of mind or an outstanding bottle of wine that transforms a meal into a sensory orgy, what you drink is an integral part of the fine dining experience. A well-executed libation can cleanse your palate and deliver a flavorful contrast or complement to your meal. A cocktail or glass of wine can also take the edge off any anxiety you have about aloof waiters or menus written in French. Enhancing your meal is the whole point of finding something stellar to drink, but diners beware: What you choose and how much you suck down can also drown a fine dinner.

Your first major hurdle is choice. What *should* you drink? Even with a grand assortment of grown-up cocktails to choose from and a seasoned bartender at your disposal, you may find yourself ordering The Usual before dinner, simply because you don't know what or how to order anything else. You also have the wine list, a dizzying volume of unpronounceable châteaus, unfamiliar wines, dates that mean nothing to you, and prices that go from cheap to trust fund.

What should you drink? *Whatever you want.* The beauty of so much choice is that you don't need to know much to know what you like. You can stand by your favorite cocktail without venturing into the unknown, but that shouldn't stop you from expanding your bar repertoire. Won't you feel just a bit savvier if you understand the difference between ordering a drink "neat" versus "straight up"? Or why clear spirits make better aperitifs and dark spirits are good digestifs? It's easy enough to remember that brandy is dry and fiery and ports are sweet, and what makes a martini European or American. The fact is, drinking doesn't require a degree in mixology or oenology. All you need is the vocabulary to articulate what you like, which you'll find here.

Now, for the obvious but oft-forgotten advice: Don't get loaded at dinner. It's easy to go overboard, whether you're celebrating a major occasion or because you're nervous and feel out of place in a high-end restaurant. But a snootful of even the best booze will skew your judgment and senses. After one too many, $200 won't seem like much for a spoonful of beluga caviar—which you probably won't even taste—and having a slurred conversation with the diners at the next table might seem like a grand idea. Along with obliterating your taste buds and good common sense, knocking back more hooch than you can hold screams "amateur." The standard markup on wine and liquor in a restaurant is *at least* two to four times the cost. And a good buzz tends to make people thirsty for more and very generous. In other words, restaurants make their money on alcohol. Unless you're dancing on tables or passed out in your banquette, your server won't cut you off or try to dissuade you from ordering a $20 thimble of Porto. Remember this and you'll save a bundle.

So pace yourself. You know your limits. If you're tucking into a seven-course meal, figure out how many drinks you can handle without getting hammered. Spread those drinks out, reserving one or two glasses for the longer main course, and order a bottle of sparkling water to pour between drinks. Or, be a teetotaler. Whether you're on a tight budget or avoiding alcohol, there's no shame in bypassing booze. Just don't order coffee with dinner. A bottle of sparkling water or a virgin juice cocktail from the bar won't overpower your meal. Some restaurants even offer full-course nonalcoholic pairings.

Bottom line: If there's one way for a Mere Mortal to ace the fine dining scene, it's by keeping your wits about you and staying slightly more sober than your companions.

How to Say "Cheers" in Five Languages

A votre santé [ah VO-truh SAHN-tay] - French
Salud [sahl-OOD] - Spanish
Cin cin [cheen cheen] - Italian
Prost [PROHST] - German
Kampei [KAHM-pie] - Japanese

Aperitifs: Classic Cocktails to Prime the Palate

Don't let the froufrou French pronunciation get you. An aperitif (ah-pehr-uh-TEEF) is nothing more than the first drink of your meal—a light liquid appetizer meant to stimulate hunger and wake up your taste buds. You can drink whatever you like, but consider that high-alcohol spirits like bourbon or whiskey and sweeter cocktails (those fruity pink umbrella drinks) or fortified wines like port have the opposite effect on your palate. Aperitifs are traditionally cold, dry, and light, such as the classic martini and other cocktails made with white spirits (vodka, gin, rum, vermouth), Champagne, and dry white wine.

EAT THIS

The word *aperitif* comes from the Latin root *aperire*, "to open."

COCKTAIL LINGO: VOCABULARY FOR DRINK LOVERS

Spirit/liquor: the liquid from a fermented grain or fruit (those that produce beer and wine, such as barley, apples, grapes) that has been distilled (boiled and vaporized). Bourbon, brandy, gin, rum, rye, Scotch, tequila, vodka, and whiskey (usually spelled *whisky* by Canadians and Scots) are spirits.

Liqueur/cordial: a sweetened spirit flavored with fruit, herbs, roots, seeds, nuts, and so forth, such as amaretto (apricot pits and almonds), Cointreau (orange peels), Chambord (black raspberries), Kahlúa (coffee beans), and ouzo (anise).

Fortified wine: a wine with a spirit (usually brandy) added, which increases the alcohol content and generally makes the wine sweeter, such as port, sherry, Madeira, and Marsala.

Highball: any spirit served with ice and soda water, or other carbonated beverage, such as tonic water, seltzer, or ginger ale; also a type of drink glass.

Neat: straight from the bottle to the glass, no shaking, no ice.

Up/straight up: shaken or stirred with ice, strained, and served in a chilled glass.

On the rocks: shaken with ice, strained, and served over ice.

With a twist: served with a ribbon of citrus rind, such as lemon, lime, or orange.

Over: one or two spirits are poured over ice, but not shaken, stirred, or chilled beforehand.

Dirty: with a splash of olive juice.

Dry: little or no vermouth, usually referring to gin or vodka martinis. In wine, *dry* means there is no hint of sugar or sweetness.

Wet: with vermouth.

CLASSIC APERITIFS BY CUISINE

French

Dubonnet rouge and **blanc** are fortified wines that are either slightly sweet with quinine flavors (red) or a dry vermouth style (white). Served on the rocks with a lemon twist.

Lillet blanc and **rouge** are mildly bitter fortified wines with citrus and vanilla or honey flavors. Served over ice with club soda, or with an orange twist.

Martinis in Europe are straight vermouth, such as Martini Rossi red (sweet) or white (dry), served on the rocks with a twist.

LAGNIAPPE

In the United States, the classic martini is a gin and vermouth cocktail served straight up or on the rocks, dry, dirty, or with a twist. Vodka martinis are the less flavorful and hangover-prone variety. Ask for an "American martini" in Europe.

A Martini Drinker's Motto

I like to have a martini
Two at the very most.
Three I am under the table.
Four I am under the host.
—DOROTHY PARKER

Pastis is a clear, anise-flavored (similar to licorice) liqueur, traditionally mixed with water and/or served on the rocks.

TALES OF THE FEAST

Absinthe, an emerald green anise-flavored liqueur made with distilled wormwood, was banned in France in 1915 because wormwood was found to contain a toxic chemical that caused neurological damage. The two major producers of absinthe at the time—Pernod and Ricard—omitted wormwood from the process and pastis, the favored drink of southern France, was born.

Italian

Bellinis are dry white or sparkling wine cocktails mixed with peach puree or juice.

Campari is a bitter red spirit with orange flavors. Served chilled with soda and a lemon twist.

Cin-cin is a cocktail of red (sweet) and white (dry) Cinzano, a famous brand of Italian vermouth. Served on the rocks.

Spanish

Sherry is a fortified wine that can be dry or sweet. Fino and amontillado, the driest styles, make the best aperitifs. Served straight up or neat.

Sangria is red wine infused with fruit, juice, and club or citrus soda, and sometimes brandy. Served with fruit, straight up, or with ice.

GRAPE EXPECTATIONS

For the Mere Mortal, selecting wine is probably the most anxiety-stoking aspect of fine dining. Most of us assume we don't know enough about wine, and worry that waiters and sommeliers are trained to prey on our amateur insecurities to nudge us into more expensive or less sophisticated bottles. Because wine can be such a touchy and intimidating subject, it seemed worthy of its very own chapter. Everything you need to know to kick-start your wine education—from learning to describe wines you like and pairing food and wine to understanding grapes, regions, and labels—is in Chapter 5, Wine: Uncorked.

Digestifs: The Sweet and Lowdown on After-Dinner Drinks

When we think of after-dinner drinks, most Americans think coffee. Maybe a latte or an espresso if you're feeling fancy. Yet there's a whole world of postprandial liquors, brandies, and dessert wines to choose from, and you don't have to be a pipe-smoking, tweed-wearing wonk to drink them. Not only are some digestifs (dee-zheh-STEEFS) thought to aid digestion (thus, the name), these drinks are sippers—made for lingering over dessert and designed to lull you out of your postmeal coma. For this reason, after-dinner drinks tend to fall in the warm, sweet, heavy, and dark category, like brown spirits (whiskey, Cognac, bourbon) and fortified wines (Sauternes, sherry, port, Madeira).

Port, or Porto, is a sweet fortified red wine made by adding brandy to wine during fermentation. Although inexpensive port-style wines are made in many countries, true Porto is made only in the Douro region in Portugal from mostly obscure varieties of grape not grown outside of the country. Quality knockoffs are made in other countries, but if the bottle doesn't say Porto (with the *o*), it's not the real thing. **Wood port** is ready to drink as soon as it is bottled and is, therefore, less expensive. It comes in two varieties: dark and fruity ruby port and the lighter tawny port, which has a smoother, nutty, dried-fruit flavor. **Vintage port**, made only from grapes grown in vintage years, is sweet and fruity with some chocolate flavors. It must be aged in wood for a minimum of one or two years and bottle-aged ten to thirty years before it is ready to drink.

Drink port with . . . a blue-veined cheese (particularly Stilton) and walnuts. Porto is also a good match for rich desserts with caramel flavors, like crème brûlée and tarte tatin (apple tart), or dark chocolate desserts. Vintage varieties are traditionally paired with foie gras.

Sherry is also fortified wine, but the brandy is added *after* fermentation takes place, giving the wine its characteristic dryness—unless it is later sweetened to make cream sherry. It is produced in Andalucia, a sunny region in southwestern Spain, from Palomino, Pedro Ximénez, and Muscat grapes. There are six important styles of sherry: **Manzanilla** is pale, light, tangy, and very dry. Light-bodied and dry **fino** is best served young and chilled. **Amontillado** is amber-colored, nutty, and dry to medium-dry. **Oloroso** is deep brown with raisiny flavors and dry to medium-dry. **Cream** sherry is sweetened oloroso, which produces a light brown, sweet, and rich digestif. **Pedro Ximénez** (PX) is very sweet and syrupy.

Drink sherry with . . . traditional tapas-style dishes, like briny olives, hard Spanish cheeses, nuts, and cured meats, particularly fino, manzanilla, and oloroso (which are also ideal aperitifs). Amontillado is often served with light or cream-based fish soups. Pedro Ximénez pairs well with blue cheese (particularly the Spanish cheese Cabrales), sweet pastry, dark chocolate, and dried fruits, but it is a transcendent treat poured over vanilla ice cream.

Brandy is made by distilling (heating and concentrating) wine or any other fermented fruit juice. Derived from the Dutch word *brandewijn* or "burnt wine," this aptly named spirit can be rich and smooth, but it's the bone-dry, fiery finish that makes people love it or hate it. **Fruit brandy,** which is also called *eau de vie* (oh duh VEE) or "water of life," is made from fermented and distilled fruit juice, including the well-known French Calvados (apple), framboise (raspberry), and Kirsch (cherry). **Grape brandy** is distilled wine. For connoisseurs, double-distilled Cognac and single-distilled Armagnac, which are aged in oak barrels for several years, are the top-notch grape brandies of the world. Other brandies may copy the Cognac style (little if any "armagnac" is made elsewhere), but the authentic stuff is produced only in southwestern France in and around the towns of the same name.

Cognac Grades

After-dinner drink menus featuring a large selection of Cognacs usually list a symbol or set of initials that indicates the age of the youngest Cognac blended in the brandy, but the precise number of years the grades represent varies from producer to producer.

*** (three stars) and V.S. (very superior): aged at least two and a half years, but usually four to seven years, depending on the producer.

V.S.O.P. (very superior old pale) and V.O. (very old): aged at least four and a half years, and up to fifteen years.

Napoleon, X.O., Extra, or Reserve: aged at least six years, and up to twenty to forty years. It is the oldest brandy made by the producer.

Drink Cognac or Armagnac with . . . dark chocolate or a fat cigar. Fruit brandies like Calvados are traditional aperitifs, served neat.

Madeira, from the Portuguese island of the same name, is a fortified wine that is heated and oxidized (exposed to air), then aged in wooden barrels. **Sercial** is the driest, and is usually served as an aperitif. **Verdelho** is nutty and smooth. The sweetest, **Bual/Boal** and **Malmsey**, are full-bodied digestifs.

Marsala, a Sicilian fortified wine, can be dry to sweet and is sometimes flavored with almonds, coffee, chocolate, or fruit. The best Marsalas, such as Vergine, are aged at least five years.

Dessert wines are made all over the world from *Botrytis cinerea*–infected or late-harvest Gewürztraminer, Riesling, Sauvignon Blanc, Semillon, and Muscadelle grapes. Many of these wines are labeled or described as "sweet," "off-dry" (semisweet), or, if they're German, "Spätlese" (sweet, late-harvest), "Beerenauslese" (very sweet, late-harvest), or Trockenbeerenauslese (very, very sweet, late-harvest). Sauternes (soh-TEHRN) is a sweet, golden dessert wine made in the Bordeaux region from Semillon and Sauvignon Blanc grapes infected with noble rot. The most famous, Château d'Yquem (sha-TOH d'ee kehm), comes from the Graves district in Bordeaux, along with other great Sauternes.

Raisin' Dessert Wines

Noble rot, or *Botrytis cinerea,* is a fungus that attacks and dehydrates grapes on the vine, which concentrates the sugar in the fruit. Wines made from these grapes are characteristically rich and sweet, like Sauternes and other dessert wines. **Late-harvest** refers to wines made from grapes left on the vine longer, a method that, like noble rot, concentrates the sugars and makes the wine sweeter.

Drink dessert wine with . . . Roquefort cheese and desserts that contrast the honey-sweetness of Sauternes, like citrus-tinged cakes, fruit tarts, poached fruit, and crème brûlée. Sauternes is also served with salty, rich foie gras. Wine should always be sweeter than the dessert it is served with.

Abstaining for Epicures: What to Drink if You're Not Drinking

For teetotalers, designated drivers, and moms-to-be, finding a grown-up nonalcoholic drink to pair with an expensive meal doesn't mean you're limited to faux-fancy standbys like overpriced sparkling water served up in a martini glass with a twist. Although it's a relatively new trend, some of the country's top restaurants, including French Laundry in California, Charlie Trotter's in Chicago, and Per Se in New York, have started offering a full-course nonalcoholic beverage pairing with top-shelf teas, juices, and sodas, handmade infusions, and specialty milk. Whether you're on the wagon or dining with people who don't drink, if there's a special occasion when you might want a nonalcoholic beverage pairing, call the restaurant ahead of time to ask if it's an option. They might put one together for you—for a fee, of course. Or make your own pairing by matching a beverage that complements (as opposed to contrasts) your meal.

"With nonalcoholic pairings, you really only want to attempt complementary pairings, like ordering a green tea to go with a green tea–marinated fish, or whole, fatty milk to go with a rich, creamy pasta course."
—PAUL ROBERTS, master sommelier,
French Laundry, Yountville, California

BE A BUFF

The Aperitif Companion: A Connoisseur's Guide to the World of Aperitifs, by Andrew Jones; *After-Dinner Drinks: Choosing, Serving and Enjoying,* by John Beckman; *The Bar: A Spirited Guide to Cocktail Alchemy,* by Olivier Said and James Mellgren

5

WINE: UNCORKED

TAKING *baby* **STEPS** *in your* **WINE EDUCATION**

A Wine Beginner's Prayer
Yea, though you walk through the valley in the shadow of grapes,
you shall fear no wine,
for your sommelier art with you.

If you don't know much about wine, flipping through a wine list the size of a phone book can be one of the most unnerving experiences of dining in a fancy restaurant. We're conditioned to believe that we need an encyclopedic grasp of geography, climate, grapes, vintages, vineyards, and wine-making—never mind the fruity lingo—to fully understand the complex world of wine. What's worse, the people who know the most about wine tend to speak a pretentious, flowery, and indecipherable language, which makes it even more difficult for the rest of us to enjoy wine unself-consciously.

Part of the reason we get so worked up about ordering wine is the popular but misguided belief that there's a right and a wrong when it comes to food-wine pairings. Red wines with red meat, white wines with chicken and seafood, and all that jazz. The truth is, there are no black-and-white rules for pairings. Plus, for every bit of wine wisdom you pick up, like "Sauvignon Blanc goes with roast chicken," there are zillions of exceptions. The aromas, flavors, and style of a wine can change depending on how and where it is produced, including the amount of sun, the slope, the climate, and the dirt the grapes are grown in—what wine nerds call *terroir* (tehr-WAHR).

For now, let's try to forget the fact that some sommeliers and wine geeks can make ordering wine seem like the ultimate Mensa litmus test. Guess what? You don't need special sensory superpowers or a particularly refined palate to learn a thing or two about wine. At the Mere Mortal stage, your mission is to score a great bottle of wine at a price you can afford, whether you pick it yourself or get help from the sommelier. No one expects you to become an overnight wine pro. Because here's the big, bad secret that wine snobs never tell you: In the early stages of your wine education, choosing a bottle is usually a shot in the dark. You learn by trial and error. If you think of understanding wine as an infinite adventure in tasting, you will slowly gather the information you need to make more informed choices. Eventually, you will bask in the glow of your good picks and learn not to fear wine lists or sommeliers.

Whether you always ask for help and take recommendations or approach your wine education as a gradual work in progress, stay true to the wines you enjoy and don't be cowed into drinking the "right" wines with your meal. If there is one Golden Rule of Wine, it's this: *If you like it, it's good.* The difference between a great wine and a bad wine depends on the person drinking it.

911 for Wine Novices: Calling in the Professionals

For some of us, poring over epic wine lists and speaking the fancy jargon will never be the fun part of fine dining. Don't get panicky or embarrassed about your weak knowledge of wine. Be honest. Follow these ridiculously simple guidelines and you'll feel like a savvy wine consumer even if you don't know Cabernet from Merlot.

- **Chat with the sommelier.** They're paid to know what you don't, and most of them are not out to gouge you. They love their job (*hello,* who wouldn't?) and get a kick out of introducing people to wine, so if you ask questions and mention the basic style of wine you like, or even the specific brand you usually drink, they can steer you in the right direction.

- **Don't fish for a recommendation.** Asking the sommelier, "What's your favorite wine?" is like asking the mother of five, "Which kid is your favorite?" They'll never admit it. Plus, what appeals to your sommelier's palate might not please yours. Instead, ask for suggestions based on your meal, the style of wine you like, or a particular brand you're familiar with.

- **Set a wine budget.** Otherwise, ordering wine can feel like psychological warfare: You spend most of the meal wondering, "Do they think I'm cheap?" or "Do I look like a sucker?" Tell the sommelier, "I'd like to spend around $50 for a bottle." If you don't want to broadcast your budget, point to a reasonably priced bottle on the list and ask, "Is there something in this range you can recommend to go with our meal?"

- **Pour your own wine.** Even the best waiters aren't above topping off wineglasses to empty bottles faster (and encourage you to order more). Waiters will also finish the bottle before getting to the table's oenophile because wine types are more likely to order another bottle. Tell your waiter, "I like to keep track of how much I'm drinking, so if you don't mind, we'll do the pouring."

What's Your Wine Type? Picking for Your Pleasure

Even if you leave the selection to the professionals or the wannabes at your table, you need to know how to describe the basic characteristics or styles of wine you like to get the best recommendation.

- **Red or white?** Everyone has a preference, and don't be swayed by old red/white food-pairing rules. There are plenty of flexible wines of both hues that go with a variety of foods, so name the one you drink most often or you're in the mood for without worrying too much about whether it goes with what you're eating.

- **Light or heavy?** The "body" of the wine is what it feels like in your mouth. Wines can be light-, medium-, or full-bodied and, generally, the weight of the wine should match the weight of the food you're eating.

- **Crisp or soft?** Whether you like more acidic wines or mellow varieties, the sommelier can quickly narrow the options if you can describe the feeling the wines you like leave on your tongue.

- **Fruity, spicy, herbal, or earthy?** Relax. You don't need really to know this much, but it helps if you can attach some other word to describe the wines you usually drink. These four words are broad enough to cover most aromas and flavors associated with wine.

The In-Crowd Wines: No-Brainers Everyone Knows

Learning about wine is like studying the social order in high school. There are freaks and geeks who memorize the most obscure details about grapes, vintages, and terroir, and there's the clique that just wants to drink it, have a good time, and not think too much.

This is the cheerleader and football-player version of what you need to know: the most popular and common wines you'll find on restaurant wine lists, their basic styles, and beginner food-pairing suggestions. Keep in mind that the overall style of the wine will change according to where the grapes are grown and how the wine is produced.

WINE CRASH COURSE

Top Whites	Style	Food Match
Chardonnay/ white Burgundy	Medium- to full-bodied, dry	Shrimp, scallops, snapper, bass, grilled salmon, grilled tuna, cod, halibut, swordfish, lobster, duck
Sauvignon Blanc	Light- to medium-bodied, dry, acidic	Sole, flounder, clams, oysters, roast chicken, mild cheeses, goat cheese
Pinot Gris/ Pinot Grigio	Light- to medium-bodied, dry, acidic	Crab cakes, quiche, prosciutto and melon, garlic, vegetable risotto, escargot, smoked fish, pâté, foie gras, oysters, shell-fish
Riesling	Light-bodied, medium acidity, and, depending on the style, dry to sweet	Spicy ethnic foods, smoked fish, mild cheeses, caviar, foie gras, sushi
Top Reds	Style	Food Match
Cabernet Sauvignon	Medium- to full-bodied, dry, tannic	Grilled or roasted red meat, such as beef and lamb, pork chops, tomato sauces
Pinot Noir/red Burgundy	Light- to medium-bodied, dry, medium tannins	Salmon, ham, pork, very rare beef or beef in cream sauce, flank steak, goose
Merlot	Full-bodied, high alcohol, dry, soft tannins	Pork chops, veal, game birds and meat, pasta in red sauce, chocolate
Syrah/Shiraz	Medium- to full-bodied, dry, peppery, tannic	Barbecued and grilled meats; dark, oily game meat
Zinfandel	Full-bodied, high alcohol, dry, soft	Steak au poivre, turkey, glazed duck, pheasant, beef stews

Name That Wine

When you order wine, it's helpful to know that wines can be named three different ways:

1. By varietal, the name of the grape the wine is made with, such as Pinot Noir, Chardonnay, or Cabernet Sauvignon.

2. By appellation, the name of the legally designated region the grapes are grown in, such as Burgundy or Bordeaux in France, Chianti in Italy, or Rioja in Spain.

3. By brand, a proprietary or trademarked name chosen by the producer that usually contains a blend of grapes, such as Opus One or Conundrum.

How to Define a Wine: Sounding Like a Wine Snob

If you learn nothing else, knowing four very basic wine characteristics—body, acidity, tannins, and sweetness—is enough to help you make solid pairing choices. It also gives you the vocabulary to tell the sommelier what you like. But don't worry. Describing wine is like talking about food. If you can take a bite of lamb chop and call it heavy and rich, you can take a sip of Pinot Grigio and call it light and acidic.

BODY

Just like a bite of fish is airy and light in your mouth and steak feels heavier (even if both bites are the same size), wines can be defined by their sense of weight: **light**-, **medium**-, or **full-bodied**. Wines may fit into more than one category because they change according to how they are produced and where the grapes are grown (that terroir again). If the wine list doesn't offer an adequate description, ask the sommelier, "What style is this wine?"

Light-bodied Wines

WHITE: Pinot Grigio, Riesling, Sauvignon Blanc, Chablis, Muscadet, Soave

RED: Burgundy, Chianti, Pinot Noir, Beaujolais, Bardolino, Barbera, Valpolicella

Medium-bodied Wines

WHITE: Bordeaux, Chardonnay, Gewürztraminer, Sauvignon Blanc, Pouilly-Fumé, Pinot Grigio, Sancerre

RED: Bordeaux, Burgundy, Cabernet Sauvignon, Merlot, Pinot Noir, Chianti Classico, Côtes du Rhône, Rioja, Syrah/Shiraz, Zinfandel

Full-bodied Wines

WHITE: California and Australia Chardonnay, Meursault, Viognier, Puligny-Montrachet

RED: Bordeaux, Cabernet Sauvignon, Merlot, Barbaresco, Barolo, Châteauneuf-du-Pape, Syrah/Shiraz, Zinfandel

ACIDITY

All wines contain acid, but when a wine produces a distinct twinge on the sides of your tongue and cheeks, it is considered acidic. Used mainly to describe whites and a few lighter reds, acidity can be low (soft, fat, or flabby), medium, or high (crisp). When ordering, consider that acidic wines (1) become less intense with salty and sweet foods, (2) can make salty foods taste saltier, and (3) cut through rich, creamy foods—all examples of a contrast wine-food pairing.

Acidic wines: Chablis, Pinot Grigio, Pouilly-Fumé, dry Riesling, Sancerre, Sauvignon Blanc, Soave

TANNINS

Typically associated with reds (or whites aged in new oak), tannins are the plant compounds found in grape skins, pits, and stems that trigger a drying sensation on your tongue and cheeks when you drink some wines. Red wines are fermented with grapes, skins and all—unlike white wines, which are fermented skinless—so they are naturally more tannic. Because tannins mellow with age and also keep bacteria at bay, tannins act as a preservative in wines, keeping the bad stuff out and softening the feel of the wine over time. Generally, the more tannins in a wine, the more likely it is to age well. Wines that are too young, with excessive tannins, may be called "tannic" or "astringent," a wine with good tannins "firm," and one with easy or low tannins, "supple" or "velvety."

SWEET VS. DRY

Not to be confused with descriptions of fruit aromas or flavors, a wine's sweetness (or lack thereof) is determined by whether or not you detect any hint of sugar on your tongue. A wine can be sweet, off-dry (with a little sweetness), or dry, which is the opposite of sweet and means your tongue won't pick up any presence of sugar in the wine. When pairing with food, remember that sweet and off-dry wines tend to go well with salty and spicy ethnic foods and dessert, but sweetness is not a good match for tart, bitter foods or buttery, creamy fare.

AROMAS AND FLAVORS

What do hints of cucumber, a breeze of jasmine, shoe leather, tar, and cat pee all have in common? They're all part of the endless rainbow of terms used to describe the aromas and flavors in wine. Wine snobs may get their hypersensitive noses bent out of shape about this next statement, but if your immediate goal is simply to pick a great bottle of wine to go with your meal, the lofty descriptions in some wine menus can distract you from an otherwise simple process of elimination. Do you know if raspberry notes will go with your *boeuf bourguignonne*? Once you've tasted the wine, will you feel like you're getting ripped off if you can't detect the lychee fruit flavor promised in its description? While there are some standard tastes and scents connected with grapes and wines (like the inevitable association of butter and toast with California Chardonnays or black pepper in Australian Shiraz), you may not pick up on some of these subtle flavors and aromas at first. It takes time— sometimes years, sometimes never—and many, many bottles of wine to hone your senses. It may be fun to play guess-that-aroma-or-flavor once the bottle arrives, but don't base your wine choice on a verbose description.

In the meantime, all you need to know are four rudimentary aroma/flavor adjectives: **fruity**, **spicy**, **herbal**, and **earthy**. Think of "fruity" as the impression you would get if you walked through a farmer's market during the peak season for berries, melons, stone fruits, and citrus. Close your eyes, whip open the spice cabinet, and take a big whiff. Smell the cloves, nutmeg, allspice, and pepper? That's "spicy." For herbal essences, think: spring, green, herb garden (basil, oregano, rosemary). Earthy? Damp soil or wood, mushrooms, wool, and minerals. Wine windbags may get carried away describing foxy, jammy, and stalky aromas and flavors, but your senses are sharp enough to know "fruity" from "herbal." When you drink wine you like, think about which category it might fall in, and share this info with your sommelier.

LAGNIAPPE

If a wine list reads more like a case study in annoying human behavior, ignore the description altogether. Dissertations about wines that are naive, flirty, promiscuous, boisterous, or mild-mannered say more about the person writing the wine list than anything useful about the wine. Wine types even have a name for this style of wine talk: purple prose.

WINE AND WOOD

Some of the best wines are aged in oak barrels, but you will also see the term *oak* used in wine descriptions, particularly for Chardonnay. The best barrels for aging wine in are made from American or French oak, but because the wood is so expensive, many cheap wines are soaked in oak chips or otherwise manipulated (or "oaked") in an attempt to reproduce the same effect of oak barrels. This technique isn't popular with vino pros, who gripe about the artificial and overwhelming effect the treatment has on a wine, so beware descriptions of "oaky" wine. It's not always a good thing.

EAT THIS

"Limousin" oak barrels, named for the forest in France where the oak grows, are considered to be the best for aging white wines and Cognac.

The Dynamic Duo: Two Principles for Pairing Wine and Food

There are two excruciatingly simple ways to match wine and food. A **complementary** pairing is one where characteristics in the wine match some of the qualities in the food, such as pairing an acidic, citrusy Pinot Grigio with a citrus-marinated or -sauced fish. A **contrast** pairing matches an opposite characteristic in the wine and food—which enhances the flavor in both—such as drinking a sweet, rich dessert wine like Sauternes with a salty, piquant blue cheese like Roquefort. If you know the basic characteristics of a wine (body, acidity, tannins, sweetness) you can decide whether it will make a tasty complement or contrast to your meal. When making a match, consider the sauce, spicing, and preparation, not just the type of meat, fish, or vegetable.

COMPLEMENTS

A good complement echoes some of the characteristics shared by the food and wine (although it doesn't always work).

Match: Body
Light-bodied wines are a good call when ordering lighter food, such as Sauvignon Blanc with a delicate fish like sole or flounder. Flavorful, heavy fare like lamb or steak won't overwhelm or be overwhelmed by a full-bodied Bordeaux or Shiraz.

Match: Sweetness
Sweet wines and desserts were made for each other. The basic rule: Wine should be sweeter than dessert. Demi-sec Champagne and sparkling wines pair with berries and apple or pear tarts; Sauternes with crème brûlée; port with dark chocolate; sherry with dried fruits; and late-harvest Riesling with peach, cherry, or plum-based desserts.

Match: Acidity
Acidic red and white wines, like Chianti and Sauvignon Blanc, are the best match for acidic, tomato-based sauces.

Match: Aromas and Flavor
Oysters have a mineral flavor that makes them an ideal partner for the mineral qualities in Sancerre, Champagne, or French Chablis. Wines described as citrusy likewise go well with sauces and dishes that feature lemon, orange, or other citrus fruit.

Mismatch: Tannins
Sometimes complementary pairings don't work. Foods high in tannins, like walnuts, apples, grapes, and other berries (things that might show up in salads, stuffings, or sauces), turn bitter and astringent with tannic wines like Cabernet and Bordeaux. Overtly

salty or sour dishes that dry or pucker the mouth (such as pickled foods and olives) also don't get along with tannic wines.

CONTRASTS

A contrast pairs opposite qualities in the wine and food, which can bring out the best in both by enhancing or toning down those differences. But sometimes opposites don't attract.

Match: Tannins

Like adding milk to tea, rich, high-protein meats have a softening effect on tannic wines—Bordeaux with a fatty roast lamb, for example, or Cabernet Sauvignon with tender filet mignon.

Match: Sweet or Dry

Sweeter, fruity wines provide a good contrast for salty and spicy fare. Dry and off-dry Gewürztraminer and Riesling tame the spice in fiery, tangy Indian and Asian dishes. Sweet Sauternes is a classic pairing for rich, savory foie gras. Vintage port is a natural foil for salty, pungent blue cheeses like Roquefort and Stilton.

Match: Acidity

The light to medium body and crisp, acidic nature of Sauvignon Blanc, Sancerre, and Pouilly-Fumé help to cut through dishes featuring thick cream sauces like Mornay and béchamel, and rich, heavy numbers like terrines and pâté. Any time you're ordering a dish that's thick, creamy, oily, or fatty, a light, acidic wine will lighten the overall impact of the food.

Mismatch: Body

Pairing a full-bodied wine like Bordeaux or Barolo with a subtly flavored and fluffy quiche Lorraine or a light-bodied wine like Beaujolais with a heavy and rich osso buco is like wearing floaties in a tsunami. The bold will completely overwhelm the mild.

BOTTLES ALL AROUND

The trickiest part about wine-food pairings in restaurants is finding a bottle that suits the whole table. You have two options: order wine by the glass or select a light- to medium-bodied wine with a good balance of fruit and acidity. The following wines work with many dishes and won't overwhelm food, so they offer a little bit of something for everyone.

Whites: Sauvignon Blanc, Pinot Grigio/Pinot Gris, Chablis, Pouilly-Fumé, Sancerre

Reds: Pinot Noir, Beaujolais-Villages, Côtes du Rhône, Merlot

EAT THIS

A red wineglass has a larger bowl and wider mouth, allowing more air to circulate and release volatile compounds that can make wine taste harsh. The white wineglass is typically smaller so that less surface area comes into contact with air, which keeps the wine from warming too quickly. If you want to look like a wine pro, hold the stem of the wineglass—don't cup the bowl in your hand—so the heat from your hand doesn't transfer to the wine.

Flights and Tastings

If you want to try several wines with your meal instead of buying a full bottle or multiple glasses, ask if the restaurant offers **tasting** sizes, a smaller (approximately 2.5-ounce) serving of certain wines on the list. Some restaurants also offer **flights**, a tasting of three or more similar wines served together so that you can compare them. A **horizontal tasting** is a sampling of similar wines from the same vintage but different châteaus or wineries, such as tasting vintage 2000 Cabernet Sauvignons from California, Chile, and Argentina. A **vertical tasting** consists of the same wine from the same winery or château, but from different (usually consecutive) vintages—for example, 1971, 1972, and 1973 Mouton-Rothschild Bordeaux. These tastings demonstrate how the traits of a wine stay the same, or change, year after year. You may also ask the sommelier to help you choose a **full-course pairing**, a selection of different wines to go with each course.

The Six Ss of Wine Tasting:
See, Swirl, Smell, Swill, Slurp, Spit

As pretentious as the swishing and sniffing routine is when the sommelier pours the first taste, taking the time to actually look at, smell, and taste the wine not only develops your senses, it also reveals the good, the bad, and the ugly about a wine. The first sip is only to make sure the wine isn't corked or otherwise "off," so do the first four "S's" in a few seconds, then give the server a nod of approval if it's a keeper. Once your waiter disappears, you can do it all over again and take your time going through the steps, but only if you're in like-minded company or can pull it off discreetly (i.e., without looking like a pompous ass).

"It takes a grand total of ten seconds to take the first taste of wine. If you put your glass up to the light or against your tablecloth and hold the wine in your mouth for two minutes with a puzzled look on your face, you look pretentious and it makes everyone at your table squirm from embarrassment."
—GEORGE COSSETTE, co-owner, Silverlake Wines,
Los Angeles, California

It's *always* okay to ask, "May I have a small taste?" when you order a wine by the glass, but not if you are ordering a bottle. By-glass bottles are already opened, and no top-notch restaurant will refuse diners a small sip to satisfy their curiosity. If you don't like it, you can even ask for a sample of another wine, but don't push it with more than two or three tastes.

See: Holding the glass by the base or stem, tilt it slightly to look for clarity and color. Wine should look clean and clear, not hazy, which indicates that sediment in the bottle has been stirred up or the wine is contaminated. What can the shade of a wine tell you? Tannins give red wines a rich, garnet hue. Grapes grown in warm climates also produce deeper reds. As red wines age, they lose tannins and the color pales. Cooler-climate grapes generally produce lighter whites. Grapes from warmer regions make richer, yellow wines. White wines darken with age and don't age as well as reds; if a white wine looks brownish-yellow, it's probably oxidized.

Swirl: With your glass resting on the table, place your hand over the base and gently rotate it in circles so the wine swirls in your glass. This releases volatile compounds in the wine before you stick your nose in it. If the wine is high in alcohol or sugar, it will leave streaks, or "legs," on the glass.

Smell: Hold the stem, stick your nose in the glass, and inhale. Remove your nose, swirl it again, then sniff it a second time. This is when funky, off odors will make themselves known. Once you've okayed the bottle, try to identify familiar aromas.

Unless you plan on eating the cork, under no circumstances should you *sniff* the cork. By all means, *look* at it. Check for serious cracks, mold, or signs of seepage, which indicate that the wine may be oxidized or corked. But don't sniff it. All corks will smell like . . . cork.

Swill: Take a sip and roll the wine around your mouth for a few seconds, noting the standout characteristics (acidity, body, tannins, and sweetness) and recognizable aromas and flavors.

Slurp: If you're dining with wine appreciators who won't flinch at the sound, curl or rest your tongue against your top row of teeth and take in a bit of air to release more of the volatile compounds. The extra bump of air also pushes more of the wine's aroma through the "back door" of your nasal cavity.

Spit: At a true tasting, swallowing a hefty sampling of wines is a bad idea unless getting tanked is the goal. There, spitting wine into the bucket provided is totally acceptable. In a nice restaurant, swallow your first sip even if it tastes like gasoline. Wait a minute to see how the wine finishes. The best wines linger longer than others.

When Bad Wine Happens to Good People: Spotting—and Sending Back—Funky Bottles

Taking the first sip of wine while the waiter hovers over you would be pointless if it weren't for one thing: Wine goes bad. Approximately 5 percent, or one in twenty bottles of wine, are affected by cork taint, usually caused by 2,4,6-trichloroanisole (TCA), a by-product of the bleaching process corks go through to clean them. A host of other factors can ruin a wine, like being exposed to heat or oxygen. Whatever the cause, bad wine happens and it's okay to send it back. It's not the restaurant's fault, and it happens more often than you think. Just don't make a scene, or worse, suck it up because you're too embarrassed to say anything.

However, don't try to turn down a bottle of wine with the complaint, "It doesn't taste like I thought it would." That's *your* problem, not the restaurant's. It is perfectly legit to send back tainted wine, but don't order plonk (cheap table wine) and expect liquid gold. A good sommelier will probably replace any bottle to keep you happy, but it's bad restaurant karma for you.

Signs Your Wine Is Funky
Looks: hazy or cloudy, or the cork is punched above the foil or lip of the bottle.

Sounds: *Pop!* when the cork comes out, unless it's a sparkling wine.

Smells: burnt matches or rubber, basement, old cabbage, eggs, stewed tomatoes, wet cardboard.

Tastes: chemicals, vinegar, cardboard, dust, or moldy fruit.

LAGNIAPPE

Whine stoppers: Don't freak out if your sommelier busts out a screw-cap bottle of wine. Although they're synonymous with jug wines, some producers are making the switch to screw caps because they provide an airtight seal, which prevents oxidation. And, with no cork, there's no chance of the problems associated with natural and synthetic corks. Collecting screw caps isn't nearly as romantic as saving those corks. If you want a memento from the meal, ask your waiter to steam the label from the bottle.

HOW TO REFUSE A BOTTLE

Vino Verbum: *"I'm not sure about this bottle. Can we let it sit for a minute or two before you pour for the table?"*

The key here is to say this after the first sip and *before* the sommelier pours the other glasses on your table. Many wines need to breathe for a few seconds or minutes to air out the heavy aroma and flavor compounds that are packed underneath the cork. Even if you think you have an off bottle, give it five minutes—maximum—to breathe before you decide to turn it down.

Vino Verbum: *"I think this bottle may be a little off. Would you mind tasting it?"*

If the wine still doesn't taste right after breathing, ask for a second opinion. Describe what you taste in the wine. Is it musty? Vinegary? Depending on the wine and your attitude, most sommeliers will sip the wine and agree with you regardless of whether they really do. However, if you ordered a pricey bottle and the wine truly isn't bad, the sommelier may politely disagree and tell you the wine tastes the way it's supposed to. Have another sip and consider your choices: (1) You can give the wine a shot and hope it improves with food or (2) politely push for an exchange.

Vino Verbum: *"I respect your opinion, but I don't think this wine is something I'll be able to enjoy. I'd like to send it back and select a different bottle."*

At this point, unless you ordered an outrageously expensive and rare vintage, the sommelier should cave in and take the bottle away. Be gracious. Say thank you and apologize for the inconvenience to keep the exchange cordial, even if you feel like a schmuck or you're convinced the sommelier tried to pull one over on you.

To Decant, or Not to Decant?

Decanting is what sommeliers are doing when they pour your bottle of wine into a fancy glass pitcher. Both the pouring and the shape of the decanter help to aerate the wine, or let it "breathe," and it's the only way to separate the sediment that collects in the bottom of old, pricey vintages. Decanting is a time-consuming ritual, which some say only older vintage red wines benefit from, but the truth is, any wine—red or white—can improve with decanting.

Three Ways to Get Wine Smart: Understanding Labels, Regions, and Grapes

Once you know the basics—enough to ask about, order, and taste wine without feeling like a fraud—taking a few more baby steps can bump your understanding of wine to the next level.

1. KNOW HOW IT'S NAMED: OLD WORLD VERSUS NEW WORLD WINES

Selecting wine can be even more confusing when you don't know anything about the major wine regions. Why? Many wines don't advertise (i.e., print on the label) the grapes they're made with. A

California Chardonnay is obviously made with mostly Chardonnay grapes, but any white Burgundy, French Chablis, and Pouilly-Fuissé is also made with Chardonnay grapes.

Old World Wines

If this is big news to you, you're not alone. One of the most challenging aspects of learning about wine is figuring out how they're named. Old World countries like France, Spain, Italy, and Germany generally classify their wines with registered place-names, a.k.a. *appellation of origin*, which is the region where the grapes were grown. (Two exceptions to the rule: Wines from Alsace, one of the seven major wine regions in France, list grape variety on labels, and German place-name wines designate regions *and* grapes on the label.)

The United States has a similar though smaller system of American Viticultural Areas (AVAs) that sets geographical boundaries for certain wine regions. Napa and Sonoma are examples. But under the European system, these names aren't just geography. The laws also stipulate everything from the types of grapes grown and the spacing between plants to the production methods winemakers must use in each region in order for the wine to carry an appellation on the label. This place-name method is rooted in the concept of *terroir*, the French term for "soil," which, in winemaking, also encompasses the climate, sun, slope, and other elements associated with where the grapes are grown. These elements greatly affect the overall style of a wine.

Old World wines that meet the standards of each region's wine laws are given special designation status, as denoted by the following words or initials on labels and wine lists.

> **France:** Appellation d'Origine Contrôlée (A.O.C.); Vin Délimité de Qualité Supérieure (VDQS)

> **Italy:** Denominazione di Origine Controllata (D.O.C.); Denominazione di Origine Controllata e Garantita (D.O.C.G.)

> **Germany:** Qualitätswein bestimmter Anbaugebiet (QbA); Qualitätswein mit Prädikat (QmP)

Spain: Denominación de Origen (D.O.); Denominacion de Origen Calificada (D.O.C.a.)

Lost? Don't give up. For eager Mere Mortals, learning the major European regions, wines, and grapes on the following maps will give you enough know-how to browse a wine list and not feel completely out of your league.

OLD WORLD WINE CRIB SHEET

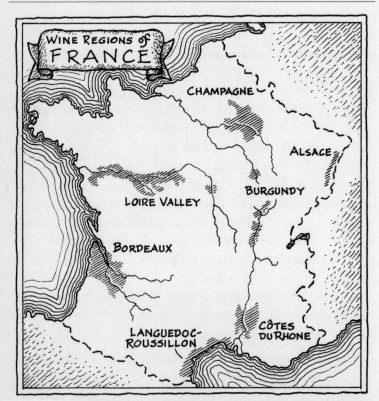

Country	Wine	Appellation	Grape
France	Riesling	Alsace	Riesling
	Gewürztraminer	Alsace	Gewürztraminer

Country	Wine	Appellation	Grape
	Bordeaux, red	Bordeaux	Merlot, Cabernet Sauvignon, Cabernet Franc, Petit Verdot, Malbec
	Bordeaux, white	Bordeaux	Sauvignon Blanc, Semillon, Muscadelle
	Sauternes	Bordeaux	Semillon, Sauvignon Blanc
	Beaujolais	Burgundy	Gamay
	Burgundy, red	Burgundy	Pinot Noir
	Burgundy, white	Burgundy	Chardonnay
	Pouilly-Fuissé	Burgundy	Chardonnay
	Maçon	Burgundy	Chardonnay
	Chablis	Burgundy	Chardonnay
	Champagne	Champagne	Chardonnay, Pinot Noir, Meunier
	Châteauneuf-du-Pape	Côtes du Rhône	Grenache, Mourvedre, Syrah, and ten other grape varieties
	Côtes du Rhône, red	Côtes du Rhône	Grenache, Syrah, Mourvedre, Carignan, and others
	Pouilly-Fumé	Loire Valley	Sauvignon Blanc
	Sancerre	Loire Valley	Sauvignon Blanc

Country	Wine	Appellation	Grape
Italy	Barbaresco	Piedmont	Nebbiolo
	Barolo	Piedmont	Nebbiolo
	Brunello di Montalcino	Tuscany	Sangiovese
	Chianti	Tuscany	Sangiovese, Canaiolo, Malvasia Bianco, Trebiano, Ciliegolo, Colorino
	Bardolino	Veneto	Corvina, Rondinella, Molinara, Barbera, Sangiovese, and others
	Soave	Veneto	Garganega, Trebbiano, and others

Country	Wine	Appellation	Grape
	Valpolicella	Veneto	Corvina, Molinara, Rondinella, and others

Country	Wine	Appellation	Grape
Germany	Mosel	Mosel-Saar-Ruwer	Riesling, Müller-Thurgau, Silvaner, and others
	Rhine	Rheingau or Rheinhessen	Riesling, Müller-Thurgau, Silvaner, and others

Country	Wine	Appellation	Grape
Spain	Sherry	Jerez District	Palomino, Pedro Ximénez, Moscatel
	Rioja, red	Rioja	Tempranillo, Grenache, Mazuelo, Graciano
	Rioja, white	Rioja	Viura, Malvasia, Grenache
Portugal	Porto	Douro	Touriga Nacional, Tinta Barroca, Touriga Francesa, and others

Grapes in the New World

For the geographically challenged, New World countries like the United States, Australia, New Zealand, Chile, and Argentina have tried to make wine easier to understand by—usually—listing the grape variety on the label. If the bottle or wine list description says it's Cabernet Sauvignon, the wine contains a majority percentage of that grape. Simple enough, right?

Naming wine by its primary grape might seem like the most obvious way to make ordering wine easier, but this method presents another problem. Remember terroir? A grape's growing environment greatly influences the characteristics of a wine. A Cabernet Sauvignon from California will not taste like a Cabernet Sauvignon from Chile, and a California Chardonnay won't taste anything remotely like Chablis, a French Chardonnay-based wine from Burgundy. Fortunately, in the grand scheme of fine wining and dining, you don't have to know the nitty-gritty about grapes and terroir. Either the wine list description or a knowledgeable sommelier can tell you all about the characteristics and style of the wine you order.

Branded Wines

Despite the hubbub about geography, some winemakers use trademarked, brand, or proprietary names for their wine—either because it is a blend of many grapes, or because it veers from appellation of origin laws. These names can be a combination of the château, the winery, and the grape variety, such as Kendall Jackson Chardonnay, or the brand and the appellation (the region the grapes were grown in), such as Mouton Cadet Bordeaux. Or, the winemaker may invent a name for the wine, such as Trilogy or Prosperity Red. **Meritage** (MEHR-ih-tihj) is a registered trademark and proprietary designation for American blends of at least two of the traditional Bordeaux grapes. **Super Tuscans** are red and white wines from Tuscany produced with nontraditional methods and grapes (like blending Cabernet Sauvignon with Sangiovese, the Chianti grape).

2. KNOW VARIETALS FROM BLENDS

Despite the heady sound of the word, a **varietal** (vuh-RI-ih-tuhl) is nothing more than a wine named for the predominant grape used to make it, such as a Chardonnay. A **blend** is a wine using several grapes, such as the classic Bordeaux blend (Cabernet Sauvignon, Merlot, Cabernet Franc) or Châteauneuf-du-Pape, which is a blend of thirteen grape varieties.

3. KNOW YOUR GRAPES

Unless you're an obsessive wine lover—and memorizing obscure grapes is sport for you—knowing the noble grapes and a few other important varieties can make wine lists easier to follow. **Noble grapes** are grown all over the world with varying degrees of success, but they hold second-to-none status in at least one classic wine region, like the Chardonnay grape in Burgundy, France.

White Noble Grapes

Chardonnay (shar-doh-NAY): This popular fruit produces dry, medium- to full-bodied wines and can be grown in most climates and soils, but France's Champagne and Burgundy regions, California, and Australia are the most noteworthy.

Sauvignon Blanc (SOH-vin-yohn BLAHN): Wines made with this grape tend to have an edgier, more acidic lightness. The best grapes are grown in Bordeaux and the Loire Valley in France, and in New Zealand and California.

Riesling (REEZ-ling or REES-ling): This German fruit is highly susceptible to noble rot, which makes wines taste sweet. The best Rieslings come from the Rheingau and Mosel regions in Germany and Alsace in France, in addition to Washington State and the Finger Lakes region in New York.

Gewürztraminer (guh-VERTS-trah-mee-ner): Known for producing big, spicy, soft wines, this cool-weather grape appears in dry wines from France's Alsace region. It is also grown in Oregon, New Zealand, and Chile.

Important White Grapes

Pinot Gris/Pinot Grigio (PEE-no GREE; PEE-no GREE-zhee-o): This is a grape with multiple personalities, depending on where it is grown. In northeastern Italy, it produces lighter, more acidic wines. In Alsace, Oregon, California, or New Zealand, the grape makes intense, perfumey, medium- to full-bodied whites that can be dry or sweet.

Semillon (say-mee-YOHN): Known for its blending powers with Sauvignon Blanc to make white Bordeaux, this grape is also grown in Australia, Washington State, and New Zealand.

Chenin Blanc (SHEN-ihn BLAHN): This grape is grown primarily in the Loire Valley to make Vouvray, an acidic, dry wine. Chenin Blanc from South Africa is called Steen.

Muscat/Moscatel (MUHS-kat/MOHS-kuh-tel): Often used in sweet dessert wines from southern France and Italy, Spain (particularly sherry), and Australia, this grape is one of the few that produces wine that actually smells like grapes.

Viognier (vee-ohn-YAY): Common in Rhône (where it's called Condrieu) and Languedoc-Roussillon in France, the Viognier grape makes rich medium- to full-bodied wines.

Grüner Veltliner (GREW-ner velt-LEE-ner): A prominent grape from Austria, Grüner Veltliner produces complex, acidic wines.

Albariño (al-vah-REEN-yo): Spain and Portugal's most-often-seen white, the Albariño or Alvarinho grape makes floral, fruity, and acidic medium-bodied wines.

Red Noble Grapes

Cabernet Sauvignon (ka-behr-NAY SOH-vihn-YOHN): Like Chardonnay, this king of red grapes thrives in many environments and is grown all over the world—including Bordeaux, California, Chile, northern Italy, Australia, South Africa, and Argentina. It produces full-bodied, tannic wines.

Merlot (mer-LOH): This grape produces softer, less tannic wines, in contrast to Cabernet-based wines. Merlot grapes dominate in blends from the "right bank" in Bordeaux, and have made a name for themselves in wines from Washington State, California, and Chile.

Pinot Noir (PEE-no NWAHR): Of the noble grapes, this one is the fussiest. It is difficult to grow and highly susceptible to weather and handling, and it is rarely blended with other grapes. It is the varietal grape in red Burgundy. Oregon, California, New Zealand, and Australia are the few other places this temperamental grape is grown with any success.

Syrah/Shiraz (see-RAH/sheer-AH): Although this grape is considered a classic—as the primary component in spicy Rhône Valley reds—its newer lineage is in Australia (labeled Shiraz), where it is often blended with Cabernet to make bold, fruity wines. It is also a major player in wines from California, Spain, Chile, South Africa, Argentina, and Italy.

Important Red Grapes

Nebbiolo (neh-b'YOH-loh): Although attempted elsewhere with less success, this grape is grown principally in Italy for two heavyweight red wines: Barolo and Barbaresco.

Sangiovese (san-joh-VAY-zeh): This is the primary Italian grape in Chianti and Brunello di Montalcino—firm, tannic wines.

Tempranillo (tem-prah-NEE-yoh): Wines made with this grape in the Rioja and Ribera del Duero regions have the most break-out potential of Spain's red grapes. It's also grown in Portugal, Australia, and California.

Zinfandel (ZIHN-fuhn-dehl): Once thought of as exclusive to California, this grape is actually a triplet—a sibling of Italy's Primitivo grape and a lesser-known Croatian grape. It produces tannic, full-bodied red and fruity white wines.

Gamay (ga-MAY): This humble grape produces light, fruity reds such as Beaujolais, which is produced in the Burgundy region and also grown in the Loire Valley.

Cabernet Franc (KA-behr-nay FRAHN): Known for its role in the Bordeaux blend, it is also used in Loire Valley wines.

Grenache (gruh-NAHSH): Used in inexpensive wines from the Rioja region in Spain, the Côtes du Rhône and Languedoc-Roussillon regions in France, and in California, this grape produces high-alcohol, supple, sweet, and fruity wines.

Vintage: Do You Care?

The short answer: no. Vintage is a fancy term that simply indicates the year a wine's grapes were harvested. If a year is listed on a bottle of wine, 100 percent of the grapes were harvested in that year. Non-vintage (NV) wines are made from a blend of grapes harvested in different years. Don't be fooled: Just because a year appears on the label doesn't necessarily mean the wine is better.

The long answer: yes. If more than one vintage is available on the list, if the wine is more than five years old or is produced in a region where weather patterns change drastically from one year to the next (Burgundy, Bordeaux, and Rhône in France and parts of Germany and Italy), or if you're about to dole out major bucks for a bottle, it's helpful to know if a restaurant is stocking the best vintages. Vintage charts can guide you, but they only rate a wine region's harvest—not individual wines.

"Most vintage questions are moot in a restaurant because only one vintage is available. When you see five to ten vintages of a particular wine on the list, there will always be someone knowledgeable on the floor who can tell you which one is ready to drink, which one is a good value, and which one they got a good deal on. Any question is fair game."

—JOE SPELLMAN, master sommelier,
Joseph Phelps Vineyards

LAGNIAPPE

Don't assume that older wine is better. A slim 10 percent of wines bottled are fit for aging in a cellar collection, and only 1 percent of wine—usually tannic, red wines like Cabernet Sauvignon and Bordeaux—is built to age for more than five years. Ninety percent of wines should be consumed within a year or two.

Label Language

Restaurant wine lists will tout the important names and places of a wine, but they may include other words that indicate a wine with special status.

Cru Classé (crew clah-SAY): *Cru* means "growth" in French, and typically refers to the 1855 classification of sixty-one top-tier châteaus in Bordeaux, which now may carry the label

Grand Cru Classé. The five elite "first-growth" châteaus, which produce wines that are labeled *Premier Grand Cru Classé,* are Lafite-Rothschild, Latour, Margaux, Haut-Brion, and Mouton-Rothschild. Vineyards in Burgundy and Champagne also use premier and grand cru classifications.

Wine List Shortcuts

- Don't order the second-least-expensive bottle on the list. It is usually the one marked up the most.

- Obscure grapes, vineyards, and hard-to-pronounce wines are usually a better value. People tend to choose familiar, big-name bulk wines (those labels you see in grocery stores), but restaurants usually have a higher markup on popular wines.

- Bordeaux sounds fancy, which is why it's more likely to be overpriced.

- Beware of huge wine-by-the-glass menus unless the restaurant is known for its tasting menu. Open bottles can sit around for days or weeks before they're finished, which alters the flavor of the wine.

- Bottles are always a better value, but by-the-glass wines are a good choice if you're dining solo or can't find a bottle to suit everyone at the table.

- House wine is never a good choice unless the restaurant is known for it or the sommelier personally vouches for the quality. Ask for a taste before you decide.

- Point if you can't pronounce. Tilt the list toward your waiter and say, "I'd like this wine."

Vins de pays (vahn deh pay-YEE): French winemakers producing quality wines that veer from A.O.C. regulations may use this classification, which means "country wine," on labels to set their wines apart from *vins de table,* or simple table wines.

Reserve: This word indicates the best wine produced by a winemaker, but in the United States and France—where there is no legal definition—anyone can slap the word on a label. Reputable winemakers still use it to distinguish their special wines. In Spain and Italy, *riserva* wines have been aged longer, which implies the wine is better.

Estate-bottled or **mis en bouteille au château/au domaine** (mee zahn boo-TAY oh sha-TOH/o doh-MEHN): The grapes were harvested and pressed, and the wine was fermented and bottled at the wine estate or château on the label.

Supérieure/Superiore: In French A.O.C. or Italian D.O.C. wines, this distinction refers to wines with a higher alcohol content than other versions of the same wine.

Classico: Italian D.O.C. or D.O.C.G. wines made with grapes grown in the heart of the wine region, usually Chianti.

Champagne and Sparkling Wine: Bubbly for Beginners

For the same reason a Bordeaux can only be from Bordeaux, Champagne with a capital *C* refers only to the stuff made in the cool northeast Champagne region in France, produced from three grapes (Pinot Noir, Pinot Meunier, and Chardonnay) using the *méthode champenoise* (may-TOHD shahm-peh-NWAZ), a process that dictates everything from planting and harvesting to blending and bottling. Bubbly made anywhere else is technically called sparkling wine. Although two red grapes, Pinot Noir and Pinot Meunier, are used in the classic Champagne blend, the skins—which deliver the color in red wines—are removed before fermentation, so the juice stays white.

Dom Pérignon was a French monk from the Abbey of Hautvillers who is credited with being the first to use a cork—instead of an oil-soaked cloth—to stopper a bottle of wine. He also invented the traditional Champagne press, which, along with his knowledge of blending, helped to perfect the art of producing white wine from red grapes.

Fantastic sparkling wines from all over the world are made using the *méthode champenoise,* and the words *Classic Method, Méthode Traditionnelle,* or *Método Tradicional* will appear on the label to distinguish these superior bubblies from the rest. About 20 percent of the sparkling wine in the United States is made in the Classic Method. Sparkling wines from elsewhere in France are called **mousseux** (moo-SEUHR), and may or may not be made using the Champagne method. **Cremant** (kray-MAHN) is a style of Champagne with less fizz, so it has a "creamier" mouthfeel. Sparkling wines from other parts of the world are called **cava** (Spain), **prosecco** or **spumante** (Italy), and **sekt** (Germany).

Occasionally, you may see the more expensive and delicate **blanc de blanc** (white from white) Champagne or sparkling wine, or the very rare **blanc de noir** (white from black) on a list. As the names suggest, they're made exclusively from white (Chardonnay) or black (typically Pinot Noir) grapes.

All Champagne and sparkling wine, like wine, should have a good balance of sweetness and acidity, but the overall style can be sweet, semidry, or dry. Because of the higher acidity, drier styles make good aperitifs, and are also a good contrast to rich appetizers or hors d'oeuvres, savory pastry, egg dishes, and oysters. Sweeter styles are a better match for dessert, particularly fresh fruit. Although they seem like the perfect couple, Champagne and most cheeses aren't ideal bedfellows because of the bubbles. Good Champagne and sparkling wine will have lots of tiny bubbles streaming up the sides of the glass; the bubbles in mediocre sparklers are bigger and float all over the glass.

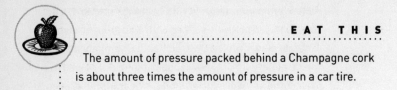

EAT THIS

The amount of pressure packed behind a Champagne cork is about three times the amount of pressure in a car tire.

CHAMPAGNE LABEL VOCABULARY

Nonvintage (NV): Champagne made from a blend of wines from different years. About 80 percent of Champagne is nonvintage.

Vintage: Grapes in the blend are grown only in the year listed on the bottle.

Cuvée (coo-VAY): Prestige Champagne made in small quantities only in vintage years with the first pressing of grapes from the highest-rated villages and bottle-aged longer than nonvintage.

Extra brut/brut nature/brut sauvage: Completely dry.

Brut: Dry.

Extra sec or extra dry: Slightly sweet.

Demi-sec: Medium-sweet.

Doux: Very sweet.

BE A BUFF

Wine Lover's Companion, by Ron Herbst and Sharon Tyler Herbst; *Windows on the World Complete Wine Course,* by Kevin Zraly; *Discovering Wine: A Refreshingly Unfussy Beginner's Guide to Finding, Tasting, Judging, Storing, Serving, Cellaring, and, Most of All, Discovering Wine,* by Joanna Simon; *The Oxford Companion to Wine,* by Jancis Robinson; *The Wine Bible,* by Karen MacNeil

6

PASTURE TO PLATE

the best of **FOUR-LEGGED, FEATHERED,** *and* **FINNED** *food*

When you eat at home or dine out in a casual restaurant, you tend to order what's quick or reliable without thinking too much about it. The main course is usually the most familiar and comforting—something you might request for your last meal—and there's no fuss over what it'll taste like or whether it's the best because you know what to expect. This is not the case in fine dining. You're paying top dollar for an experience, a meal that should be extraordinary in every way. Getting the same old chicken or salmon simply won't do. These restaurants offer cuts of meat and varieties of fish, seafood, and poultry you've probably never heard of or, maybe, felt brave enough to gamble your money on. And the chefs who handle these beauteous slabs of flesh all day long are craftsmen who know everything there is to know about their raw material: where it came from, how it should look, smell, feel, and taste, and precisely how to prepare it. You're getting the best of the best *from* the best—what better place is there to bust out of tired food habits?

But to be comfortable ordering sweetbreads or lamb shanks,

you probably want to know more about it before you put it in your mouth. The little details, like what part of the animal it comes from and what it'll look like when it shows up on your plate, can take a lot of the mystery out of the meat. As you venture into high-class cuisine and your tastes broaden, it's reassuring to know the different cuts of meat, the best ways to prepare them, and what "medium" means to a chef. If you've ever wondered what the difference is between a porterhouse and a T-bone, what tripe really is, or why beluga caviar is so damn expensive, you're about to find out. Vegetarians and vegans, skip to the next chapter.

Meat Market: A Carnivore's Guide to Beef, Pork, Lamb, and Veal

A CUT ABOVE

The meat from an animal is divided into large sections called **primal cuts**. Smaller **subprimal cuts** are sliced from these primal cuts, and even smaller cuts—usually in the form of steaks, chops, or roasts—are carved from these sections. For example, beef strip (a.k.a. short) loin is a primal cut that runs along the steer's back between the rib and sirloin sections, and is divided into two subprimal cuts: top loin and tenderloin. Filet mignon is cut from the tenderloin, and New York strip steaks are cut from the top loin. **Crosscuts** are pieces of meat carved out of more than one subprimal cut, like T-bone and porterhouse steaks, which contain meat from both the top loin and tenderloin sections.

Steaks, chops, and cuts of roast are your primary choices on a restaurant menu. **Roasts** are larger cuts that are cooked whole and carved into individual servings. **Steaks** are smaller cuts of meat (typically beef) that are cooked and served as individual portions. Pork, lamb, and veal "steaks" are typically called **chops**. Butchers may distinguish these cuts as carved exclusively from the rib or loin section of the animal, while steaks can be cut from almost any section on a cow.

GRADE EXPECTATIONS

When you're eating high on the hog (or cow, lamb, or turkey) in a restaurant, some menus may include a grade, brand, or certification label. Some of the words indicate quality standards set by the U.S. Department of Agriculture (USDA); others are virtually meaningless because they're not regulated.

The USDA uses as many as eight grades to designate the quality of different types of meat, depending on the animal, but there are only three you need to remember in a restaurant: **Prime**, **Choice**, and **Select**. Lower grades aren't served in restaurants, much less advertised on the menu.

Beef grades are based on two main components: the age of the animal and the amount of marbling in the meat. Marbling is the amount of streaky, white fat in the muscle, and the more there is, the better the grade. Extra fat might not sound like a good thing, but when meat is cooked, the fat melts into the meat and makes it more tender, juicy, and flavorful.

USDA Prime beef, lamb, and veal is the best of the bunch and, naturally, über-expensive. Only 2 percent of the beef sold in the United States makes the Prime grade, so if the restaurant is serving it, they'll flaunt it on the menu. **USDA Choice** is second best and far more common; 45 percent of beef scores this grade. Unless it's listed as Prime on the menu, chances are the lamb, veal, or beef served in fancy restaurants is (or should be) Choice grade. **USDA Select** makes up the bulk of the beef sold in the United States; lamb in this category is graded **Good.**

GREEN CUISINE LABELS

USDA-Certified Organic meat must meet National Organic Standards, which state that livestock must be hormone- and antibiotic-free, raised on 100 percent organic feed, and have access to the outdoors.

Free-range means the animal has a chance to roam outdoors every day, but USDA guidelines for using the term do not guarantee the animal actually spent time outside. If the barn door is open for a certain amount of time, the animal can be called "free range."

Natural is a USDA-regulated word that means the meat is minimally processed without the use of artificial ingredients—a loose definition that still leaves room for the use of hormones, antibiotics, and pesticides.

Heritage animals are rare and arguably tastier breeds with historical, cultural, or geographical significance. No law regulates use of the word, but it typically implies that the animal is a pure breed with a tradition in the United States and is produced by sustainable means. Many heritage breeds also have regional ties, like the Narragansett turkey native to Rhode Island or Ossabaw Island hog from Georgia. Small, local, upscale restaurants are more likely to feature heritage foods, but larger restaurants may offer them on special seasonal menus (like Bourbon Red turkey around Thanksgiving).

"The same difference of flavor exists between breeds of beef, pork, and poultry that exists in different varieties of tomato or corn. By preserving a diversity of heritage breeds, we're preserving a diversity of flavor in our foods."
—DON SCHRIDER, communication director of the American Livestock Breed Conservancy

Let's get one thing straight: Phrases like **no hormones added**, **vegetarian-fed**, **grass-fed**, **antibiotic-free**, and **no pesticides** have no legal definition. Any meat producer is free to use them. Green restaurants might list these terms on the menu, but they should also be able to tell you where the meat came from. The reputation of the farm or ranch is more important than an undefined label.

BEEF

If beef is what's for dinner, knowing where it comes from on the cow and what it'll look like on your plate is the kind of information you need to choose a cut you'll love—and you *should* love it when you're paying top dollar. The best beef comes from the center section of the steer: the rib, short loin, sirloin, and loin. These areas contain the least-used muscles, which makes for the most tender and fatty meat. Steaks and roasts cut from these sections are best cooked by quick, dry heat, like grilling, roasting, or broiling. Meat from the front and rear quarters—the chuck, round, shoulder, and leg—gets more of a workout and is tougher, which makes it ideal for cooking by slow, moist heat, such as braising, stewing, or poaching.

BUTCHER'S BLOCK	
Primal Cuts	**On the Menu**
Chuck	Chuck roast, English roast, Flatiron steak, Swiss steak, butcher's steak, petite fillet, short ribs, ground chuck, stew meat
Rib	Rib-eye, Delmonico, entrecôte, prime rib, standing rib roast, short ribs
Short loin and tenderloin	New York or Kansas strip steak, club steak, Chateaubriand, tournedos, filet mignon, porterhouse, T-bone
Sirloin	Tri-tip, coulotte steak, top sirloin steak, London broil
Round or rump	Swiss steak, Manhattan roast, Manhattan steak, kabob meat, ground round
Flank	Flank steak, London broil, ground beef
Plate	Skirt steak, hanger steak, stew meat, ground beef
Foreleg/brisket	Brisket, corned beef, shanks, stew meat

On the Plate

If you're an unabashed carnivore, ordering a nice, fat steak is a natural choice because old-school steakhouses and fine restaurants are the rare places you'll actually find USDA Prime aged beef in this country. These are the elite cuts that stand out.

Filet Mignon

Filet mignon is a thick, boneless steak cut from the tenderloin, the most tender section of beef money can buy. It's also called *filet de boeuf,* or it can be served as Chateaubriand, a French preparation for two that uses a larger cut from the center of the tenderloin and is traditionally served with béarnaise sauce.

Tournedos and **medallions** of beef are small, round, boneless slices of meat cut from the narrow end of the tenderloin—the same area filet mignon is cut from.

New York strip is a boneless steak cut from the top loin. It can also be called Ambassador steak, Kansas City steak, or just plain strip steak.

New York Strip

Delmonico steak is a strip steak with a bone cut from the top loin. It's also called club steak, shell steak, or bone-in strip steak.

T-Bone

T-bone is a bone-in crosscut that is part strip steak and part filet mignon, cut from the top loin and tenderloin.

Porterhouse steaks are T-bones with a bigger section of tenderloin attached.

Rib-eye is a boneless steak cut from the rib section. The French call it *entrecôte* (ahn-treh-KOHT).

Porterhouse

Prime rib is a steak-size portion cut from a cooked rib roast; it may or may not have a bone. Despite what the name implies, not all "prime rib" is USDA Prime. If it is, the menu description will say "USDA Prime Rib."

London broil is typically a section of flank steak. It can also be cut from the leaner, tougher top round, sirloin, and chuck sections, but flank is best.

Top sirloin, **chuck eye**, and **round tip** steaks are carved from the tenderest area of the primal cuts they're named for. Because they are tougher than other top-of-the-line steaks, chefs usually marinate these cuts to soften the meat.

How to Say "Beef" in Five Languages

Boeuf [BUHF] - French
Manzo [MAHN-dzoa] - Italian
Carne de res [KAHR-neh deh REHS] - Spanish
Gyuniku [GEE-oo-nee-koo] - Japanese
Rindfleisch [RIND-fleyesh] - German

Mad About Cow

Uncooked meat might not get the USDA's approval or sound very appetizing, but raw beef is the centerpiece of two famous delicacies: **Beef carpaccio** is an Italian appetizer made from paper-thin slices of cold, raw beef drizzled with vinaigrette and shavings of Parmigiano-Reggiano cheese. **Steak tartare** is a mound of seasoned raw ground beef topped with an egg yolk and garnished with onions, parsley, shallots, capers, and sometimes anchovies.

The Myth, the Legend: Kobe Beef

Have you heard the one about the beer-swilling, sake-massaged Japanese cows that produce the most expensive beef in the world? No, this is not a joke. People have paid more than $300 per pound for it. The mythology surrounding these sacred cows may seem far-fetched, but this is what we know: Kobe beef is a semiprotected name, like A.O.C. wines in France, applied only to beef produced in the Hyogo (formerly Tajima) province in Japan from the black Wagyu (WA-goo) breed of cattle. (*Wa* means "Japanese" and *gyu* is "cattle.") Beer mash, according to lore, was given to the animals to stimulate their appetite in the summer. Because land is expensive in Japan and the cattle had little room to roam, they were allegedly massaged with sake to soften their coats and de-stress tense muscles, which was also believed to produce more tender, fatty meat. Small ranchers from this province may have indulged their cattle years ago and farmers with only a handful of Wagyu may have the resources to coddle their cows these days. However, it's highly doubtful that commercial ranchers today dole out the beer and sake spa treatments to large herds of 1,200-plus-pound cattle.

Whether it's the TLC or the less romantic DNA (some say the breed is genetically predisposed to tenderness and marbling) that makes the beef so supreme, Kobe has earned the title of "the foie gras of beef" for its legendary soft, buttery texture. So buttery, in fact, the meat surpasses the highest standards set for the USDA Prime grade. Because the fat content of Kobe is on par with butter and ice cream, it is usually served very rare or raw. The meat will literally dissolve into a flavorless mess if it is overcooked, so it is only quickly seared if it is cooked at all.

About ten years ago, Japan briefly lifted the law restricting the export of Wagyu cattle and a few savvy American ranchers were able to import the prized breed. The restrictions are back in place today, but the breed is thriving in the United States. Cattlemen who raise Wagyu here say the only real difference between Japanese and American Kobe is in the breeding. Instead of crossbreeding Wagyu bulls with dairy cows, as is the custom in Japan, ranchers here breed Wagyu bulls with Angus cows.

Menus may or may not differentiate between American or Japanese Kobe. Although the USDA requires producers to label American Kobe beef on retail packaging, the rule doesn't apply to restaurants. Reputable establishments will call it American Kobe beef or Wagyu, or they might include the farm brand, like Big Bottom Valley or Snake River Farms American Kobe, in the menu description. Many restaurants simply call it "Kobe beef" because people aren't familiar with "Wagyu."

When Old Meat Is a Good Thing

If "aged beef" sounds like the last thing you'd want to pay top dollar for in a restaurant, you'd be wrong. Aging beef may be time-consuming and expensive, but the few restaurants offering it do so because the process turns great beef (only Prime and Choice beef can be aged) into sublime beef.

Dry-aged beef is hung, unwrapped, in temperature- and humidity-controlled rooms for up to four weeks. It is the crème de la crème of meat for two reasons: First, the aging process releases enzymes in the meat that break down muscle fibers, which tenderizes the texture of the beef. Second, the meat loses moisture and shrinks during aging, which further concentrates the flavors. Meat dry-aged for twenty-one to twenty-eight days loses up to 30 percent of its weight in the process.

Wet-aged beef uses the same technique, but the meat is vacuum-sealed in airtight plastic so there's no shrinkage—an important factor for restaurants because they get a better return on their money if the meat doesn't shrink. It also means wet-aged beef won't have the distinct, concentrated flavor of dry-aged beef. If the menu only states that the steaks are "aged" or "prime-aged," chances are the beef is wet-aged.

PORK

If pork is on the menu, it's usually in the form of a chop. **Loin** and **rib chops,** which can be boneless or bone-in, are the most tender and fatty, and are best suited to dry-heat cooking (grilling, broiling, or panfrying). **Butterflied chops** are thick cuts from the loin sliced in half but still connected, and splayed open. **Pork loin** and **center cut loin** are one- to two-inch-thick boneless cuts sliced from a whole cooked pork loin roast. (Roasts are cooked whole to keep lean sections from drying out.) These pieces of roast shouldn't be confused with **pork tenderloin**, which is like beef tenderloin—a lean, narrow sliver of tender meat that runs through the loin. Because it dries out so quickly, grilling and roasting with high, dry heat is the best way to cook tenderloin, but in restaurants, you'll also see it served as thick, coin-shaped cuts called **medallions**.

BUTCHER'S BLOCK	
Primal Cuts	On the Menu
Shoulder	Boston roast, shanks (hocks)
Loin	Tenderloin, center cut chops, loin chops, crown roast, rib chops, back ribs, Canadian bacon
Ham	Ham, ham steak, shanks, prosciutto, *jamón*
Belly	Spareribs, St. Louis ribs, bacon, salt pork

You Say Prosciutto . . .

Cured ham goes by many names depending on the country of origin. Prosciutto di Parma from Italy, *jamón serrano* from Spain, Bayonne from France, and Black Forest ham from Germany are all name-controlled (like A.O.C. wines) varieties. These famous salt-cured hams are sliced paper-thin and served with cheese boards, wrapped around melon, tossed into pasta, and more. Smoked country hams, like Smithfield ham from Virginia, Westphalian ham from Germany, and Austrian Speck, might not appear on many upscale menus, but smaller boutique restaurants focused on green cuisine may highlight these branded hams to lend an air of authenticity to the menu. Pancetta is an Italian dry-cured bacon that is served cubed in pastas, salads, or risotto, or sliced and served like prosciutto.

How to Say "Pork" in Five Languages

Cochon [koh-SHOHN] - French
Maiale [mah-YAA-lay] - Italian
Carne de puerco or *cerdo* [KAHR-NEH deh PWER-ko] - Spanish
Schweinefleisch [SHVEYEN-fleyesh] - German
Butaniku or *poku* [boo-TAH-nee-koo] - Japanese

LAMB

Loin and **rib lamb chops** are the most tender and fatty (although loin chops are leaner), and these prize cuts are always bone-in. A serving of **rack of lamb** in a restaurant isn't the whole rack; it is a section of three to four rib chops cut from the whole roast rack. Dry-heat cooking works for both, but grilling is the best method for lamb chops, and rack of lamb is better roasted. Lamb chops and racks should be ordered medium-rare to medium because the meat loses a lot of its flavor and character if it is overcooked. If pinkish meat isn't your bag, think about ordering another dish. **Frenching** is a fancy way of cutting meat away from the rib so that part of the bone is exposed. Rack of lamb, crown roast, and other large cuts are often frenched and served with frilly paper caps on the tip of the bone.

Baby lamb is less than twenty weeks old, under twenty pounds, and milk-fed, which gives the meat a light, creamy-pink hue. Once a lamb is given solid food, the meat begins to turn red. **Lamb** is usually between five months and one year at slaughter. **Mutton** is more than two years old and best in braises or stews.

BUTCHER'S BLOCK

Primal Cuts	On the Menu
Shoulder	Blade chop, stew meat, kabob meat
Rib	Rack of lamb, crown roast, rib chop
Loin	Loin roast, loin chop, medallion, tenderloin
Leg	Sirloin half-leg roast, gigot, sirloin chop, lamb shank, kabob meat
Breast/foreshank	Whole breast, foreshank, spareribs

How to Say "Lamb" in Five Languages

Agneau [ah-NYOH] - French
Agnello [ah-NYEH-loh] - Italian
Carne de cordero [KAHR-neh deh kohr-DEH-roh] - Spanish
Lamm [LAHM] - German
Kohitsuji [koh-heet-SOO-jee] - Japanese

VEAL

Veal is the centerpiece in several classic Italian dishes. **Osso buco**, or braised veal shanks (leg bones), appears on many menus, regardless of the cuisine. A long, narrow spoon is used for scooping out the marrow—the rich, meaty center of the bones that is the pièce de résistance of the dish. (Restaurants sometimes call braised lamb shank "lamb osso buco.") **Valdostana** is a breaded, sautéed veal chop stuffed with fontina cheese. **Saltimbocca** is thin slices of veal rolled with prosciutto and sage, then sautéed in butter and white wine. **Veal scallopini** is a dish of thin slices of sautéed veal drizzled with a pan sauce, such as lemon-caper *(piccata)* or mushroom-Marsala *(alla Marsala)*. **Weiner schnitzel** is a German dish of paper-thin slices of veal that are coated and fried, and served with a variety of sauces and garnishes, like sour cream–lemon–caper *(Kiserschnitzel)* or fried eggs and anchovies *(Holsteinerschnitzel)*.

Most veal comes from calves that are milk- or formula-fed and raised in small pens to prevent the delicate meat from becoming muscled and toughened. Therein lies the dilemma for some meat-eaters, not to mention most animal activists: Is it cruel to pen calves in small stalls, or is it an unfortunate reality of producing an exquisite piece of meat? If it's a matter of conscience for you, seek out green cuisine restaurants that serve grass- or range-fed veal from calves that are allowed to roam. The effect on the meat is significant: The prized mild, tender, and pale pink meat of milk-fed and penned veal turns into a red, beefy, less delicate meat when the calves feed on grass and are allowed more movement. If the menu doesn't define the style of veal being used, chances are it is the traditional milk-fed, penned variety. Don't order it if the animal's treatment is an issue.

BUTCHER'S BLOCK	
Primal Cuts	**On the Menu**
Shoulder	Braised veal, chops
Rib (rack)	Veal hotel rack, chops
Loin	Tenderloin, medallions, loin chops
Leg	Osso buco, scallopini, schnitzel, cutlets
Breast/foreshank	Osso buco, veal stew

EAT THIS

Veal has less fat than a boneless, skinless chicken breast, and 10 percent fewer calories.

How to Say "Veal" in Five Languages

Veau [VOH] - French
Vitello [vih-TEHL-oh] - Italian
Carne de ternera [KAHR-neh deh tehr-NEH-rah] - Spanish
Kalbfleisch [KAHLPS-fleyesh] - German
Koushi [koh-OO-shee] - Japanese

EATING FROM SNOOT TO TAIL

Dining on brains, tongue, or feet is hardly a matter of "waste not, want not." Whether it's ground, stuffed, sautéed, or fried, variety meat or offal—the internal organs, head, tail, and feet of an animal—is transformed into delicacies like the classic French pot-au-feu, sausages, braised oxtail, and Italian *busecca* in upscale restaurants. For the brave and uninitiated, a restaurant is the ideal place to try exotic dishes like calf's liver and sweetbreads because they're as good as they get in the hands of a skilled chef. Usually, it's the oddball, dare-you-to-eat-it dishes that chefs love to cook most. For squeamish eaters, it's worthwhile to learn the various ways these bits and pieces are prepared and how they'll appear on a menu, in case you want to avoid them altogether.

IF YOU DARE TO GO THERE		
Variety Meat	On the Menu	Popular Preparations
Brains	*Cervelles* (French) *Cervellos* (Italian) *Cesos* (Spanish)	Lamb and sheep brains, considered the best, are served fried, poached, and sautéed. Ground calf and beef brain may be used as filling in savory pies or terrines.

IF YOU DARE TO GO THERE

Variety Meat	On the Menu	Popular Preparations
Tongue	*Langue* (French) *Lingua* (Italian) *Lengua* (Spanish)	Beef, calf, lamb, and pig tongues are stewed, boiled, fried, pickled, or smoked. *Langue de boeuf à la bourgeoise,* beef tongue in red wine, is a well-known French dish.
Cheek	*Joue* (French) *Guancia* (Italian) *Mejilla* or *cachete* (Spanish)	Beef and veal cheeks—tough, muscle-y meat with a robust, beefy flavor—melt when stewed or braised.
Heart	*Coeur* (French) *Cuore* (Italian) *Corazón* (Spanish)	Beef, veal, and lamb hearts, which have a strong flavor and chewy, tough texture, are usually grilled.
Tripe	*Gras-double* or *tripes* (French) *Trippa* (Italian) *Panal, panza, cacariso* (Spanish)	The stomach lining of an animal—usually cow—has a soft, creamy, and slightly chewy texture. It is used in soups (Spanish *menudo,* Italian *busecca*); marinated and fried or grilled; or braised in wine, broth, or cider, as in the French dish *tripes à la mode de Caen.*
Sweetbreads	*Ris* (French) *Animelle* (Italian) *Mollejas* (Spanish)	Made from the pancreas and thymus (neck) glands of calves, lambs, and occasionally pigs, sweetbreads are used in gratins, braised, roasted, grilled, and poached. *Ris de veau* (veal) and *ris d'agneau* (lamb) are popular French dishes.

IF YOU DARE TO GO THERE

Variety Meat	On the Menu	Popular Preparations
Kidney	*Rongon* (French) *Rognoni* (Italian) *Riñon* (Spanish)	Young kidneys from veal and lamb are mildly flavored and, because they dry out easily, are best when quickly grilled, fried, sautéed, or braised.
Intestine	*Intestin* (French) *Intestino* (Italian) *Intestino* (Spanish)	Pig intestines are used to e-case sausage. Beef innards are used to make blood sausage (also called black pudding, or *boudin noir*).
Liver	*Foie* (French) *Fegato* (Italian) *Hígado* (Spanish)	Cooked whole, grilled, or fried and served with sauce, calf's liver (*foie de veau*) is the most delicate and popular. Pork, goose, and duck livers are used in pâtés, terrines, and sausages.
Trotters	*Pied* (French) *Piedi* (Italian) *Pie* (Spanish)	Pig feet, called trotters, are poached, braised, grilled, and fried. Calf feet are used to make stock or calf's-foot jelly.
Oxtail	*Queue de boeuf* (French) *Coda di bue* (Italian) *Rabo de buey* (Spanish)	Oxtail (skinned beef tail) has a rich, beefy flavor when it is braised and used in sauces and soups.

COOKED TO ORDER

Do you like your steak charred to a crisp or still mooing? Does pink meat strike fear in your heart, or hunger? Knowing your preference and being able to describe it to your waiter is important because your idea of medium might not sync with the chef's. If you're not sure how you want your meat cooked, defer to the kitchen; the grill chef prepares the same dish umpteen times a day and knows the ideal doneness for the meat.

Very rare meat is squishy and the center is blood red or purplish in color. Beef and lamb are the only meats you can order this way. The French call it *bleu* (BLUH). **Rare** beef and lamb is soft in the center and can be bright pink or red with blood-red areas near the bone, if there is one. **Medium-rare** is a common request for steaks, lamb, and veal chops. The meat is semisoft, pink in the middle, and browned closer to the edges with no blood-colored spots. **Medium**-cooked meat is firm and mostly browned with a little pink in the middle, which is ideal for fattier cuts of beef, lamb, and veal. **Medium-well**, typical for veal and pork, is very firm and may still have slightly pink juices running through the meat. **Well-done** is a nice way of saying "overcooked" to a top chef. At this point, any type of meat will be dry, tough, and browned throughout.

"Two things diners do that annoy the kitchen:
Ordering food well done is anguishing.
So is seasoning food before tasting it."
—RICK TRAMONTO, chef, TRU, Chicago

A Field Guide to Birds:
Capons and Grouse and Ostrich—Oh My!

Poultry is probably the one thing on a menu we understand the most about because we eat it so frequently, and it has a relatively simple body (breast, wing, leg, thigh). You know what's going to show up on the plate if you order half a roasted chicken or duck breast. What you might not be familiar with is the complete range of feathered foods that many fine restaurants serve.

Chicken is the most popular poultry in the world. **Capon** is a young chicken that has been castrated, which produces fat and tender white flesh. **Poussin** is a small, young chick without flying feathers with lean, soft, and juicy flesh. **Rock Cornish game hen** is a meaty miniature chicken with a mild flavor; it is usually cooked and served whole. Coq au vin is a classic French dish of rooster cooked in red wine with mushrooms, onions, herbs, and bacon.

LAGNIAPPE

Pasta and chicken are always cheap, but rarely a bargain. Generally, the markup on inexpensive ingredients is higher than on luxury ingredients. Example: The restaurant may charge you twenty bucks for a pasta dish that cost them $3 to make. But a $50 steak that cost the restaurant $20 is the better value.

Duck is an oilier, darker poultry with a gamey and rich flavor. **Moulard** is a large-breasted, fatty duck prized for its liver, which goes into foie gras and pâté, and for *magret de canard,* tender, thinly sliced duck breast grilled rare. **Muscovy** duck has a lean and strongly flavored flesh. **Pekin** duck, the centerpiece of the famous Chinese dish Peking duck, has a dark, rich, fatty flesh.

Goose can be either wild or farmed, and although it doesn't produce as much meat as other poultry, its rich, dark flesh and fatty skin make it perfect for roasting. The best foie gras and pâté are made from fattened goose liver.

Grouse is a wild bird beloved for its lean and distinctly flavored meat, which comes from a diet of wild herbs and vegetation specific to the region it forages in. Of several species, red grouse from Scotland is the most rare and sought-after.

Guinea hen is a light-fleshed, lean bird similar to chicken, but smaller, with reddish, mildly flavored meat reminiscent of pheasant.

Ostrich, **emu**, and **rhea** are large, flightless birds that produce very lean, dark red meat that almost looks like beef. These birds do not produce breast meat, but their tenderloin, leg, and thigh meat is cut into steaks, medallions, or roasts.

Pheasant is a game bird cousin to chicken, but with a larger breast and wilder flavor than domesticated poultry. **Partridge** are in the pheasant family, but they are smaller, more lean, and gamey tasting.

Turkey is a large wild or farm-raised bird with very lean meat. Older species of American heritage turkeys, like the Bourbon Red and Narragansett, are slowly making a comeback after being all but replaced in the industry by White Holland turkeys, which are cheaper and easier to produce, though less flavorful.

How to Say "Tastes Like Chicken" in Five Languages

Goûte semblable au poulet
[GOOT SAHM-bleh-behl oh poo-LAY] - French
Ha un sapore simile al pollo
[ah oon sah-POA-ray see-MEEL ahl POHL-loh] - Italian
Prueba similar al pollo
[proo-AY-bah see-mee-LAHR ahl POH-yoh] - Spanish
Schmecken ähnlich Hähnchen
[SHMEK-ehn AYN-likh HAYN-khen] - German
Aji onaji niwatori
[AH-jee oh-NAH-jee nee-wah-TOH-ree] - Japanese

Luxury Liver: The Facts About Foie Gras

Most high-dollar restaurants assume everyone knows what foie gras (FWAH GRAH) is, which makes the expensive and weird-to-pronounce item that much scarier if you've never had it. **Foie gras** is whole, fattened goose liver that has been soaked in milk, marinated in Armagnac, port, or Madeira, and baked. It is very rich, with a delicate, silky texture, and it is not cheap. There are less expensive varieties, such as pâté de foie gras, a puree of at least 80 percent goose liver with other fillers such as pork liver, truffle, and eggs, and mousse or puree de foie gras, which contains at least 55 percent goose liver. Duck liver, or foie gras de canard, is not as pricey and has a more rustic, earthy flavor. Traditionally, foie gras is served in terrines (small dishes coated with pork fat), eaten on buttered toast, and paired with Porto or Sauternes. It is also a component in beef Wellington, a fillet of beef covered in pâté de foie gras, wrapped in pastry, and baked.

FOIE GRAS FRACAS

For all its epicurean merits, foie gras isn't without controversy. Many object to the fact that geese and ducks are force-fed grain to fatten their livers. Those on the other side of the fence say this method only mimics in captivity what the animals do in nature: Before winter, birds in the wild gorge and get fatter for the colder months. In 2004, California implemented a delayed ban on foie gras production, to take effect in 2012, in the hopes that producers will find alternative methods of fattening their birds. Several other states, including New York and Illinois, are considering similar bans. A few marquee restaurants, like Charlie Trotter's in Chicago and San Francisco's Jardinière, are also refusing to serve foie gras.

Fish Out of Water: Netting the Best Fish, Shellfish, and Seafood

Thanks to a certain book detailing the seedy underbelly of restaurant kitchens and the life of a misfit celebrity chef, we're now painfully aware that ordering fish can be a gamble even in the best restaurants. Tales of last week's catch showing up in Monday night's special and mussels wallowing in their own murky filth are enough to turn anyone off of fish and seafood, not to mention the fact that the delicate flesh is the most vulnerable to spoilage in a restaurant. At the same time, you have to realize that not all fish and seafood is dicey, and most upscale restaurants take extreme care to protect their merchandise. If you haven't established a relationship with the restaurant, which is how you get insider information about how much turnover there is or what's fresh that day, you'll have to use a little bit of common sense when choosing fish and seafood.

Fin for Yourself

- When in doubt, order fish on Thursday, Friday, and Saturday, when fish markets and distributors do their biggest business, not Sunday or Monday.

- Politely dig for information about turnover. Avoid pointed questions like "Is the fish fresh?" Instead ask, "Where is the halibut from?" or "Do a lot of people order the mussels?" or "Is the salmon wild or farmed?" Good waiters will steer you in the right direction.

- Don't order oysters on the half-shell or raw clams if the restaurant doesn't have a raw bar. It may be fresh, but raw shellfish will have a low turnover in restaurants that don't specialize in it, and the staff may not handle it often enough to know how to spot the good, the bad, and the trip to the ER in a batch.

HEADS OR TAILS?

Fish can be served in four styles: **Fillets** are boneless sides of the fish and may or may not have skin attached. **Steaks** are vertical crosscuts sliced from a whole fish and may have a sliver of backbone running through them. **Dressed** fish is scaled with the organs, head, tails, and fin removed. **Whole** fish is scaled with the organs removed, but the head, tails, and fin are left intact. If the fish is described as "whole" on the menu, you can ask your waiter to have it "dressed" before it reaches the table.

CATCH OF THE DAY: WHAT TO EAT AND WHAT TO AVOID

Could there *be* more conflicting news about fish? We read about the great health benefits of eating the omega-3-rich flesh, but at the same time, there's news of once-abundant species being overfished or trawled into extinction as bycatch, the "incidental" goods caught in a fisherman's line that are discarded. (The United Nations Food and Agriculture Organization reports that as much as 25 percent of the fish caught is thrown away or dies as bycatch.) Never mind the alarming mercury levels discovered in certain fish. Trying to decipher what you've heard and read while you're suffering from fancy menu overload doesn't help matters. One trick: When in doubt, choose fish listed as Pacific or Alaskan versus Atlantic varieties, which are more likely to be overfished. You can make informed decisions by consulting the pocket-sized Seafood Watch guide (get a downloadable version at www.seafoodwatch.org), a frequently updated list of fish to avoid and good, safe-catch alternatives to order. Or memorize your favorites from the following list and order only what you're sure about.

THE BEST CATCH		
Fish	Texture, Color	Flavor
Catfish	Firm, white	Medium
Clams	Firm, off-white	Full
Cod (Pacific)	Delicate, white	Mild
Crabs: Dungeness, Alaskan king,* snow (U.S.*/Canada), and stone	Delicate, white	Mild
Summer flounder/fluke*	Delicate, white	Mild
Halibut (Pacific)	Firm, white	Mild
Lobster: spiny, U.S./Maine*	Medium, white	Mild
Mahi mahi/dorado*	Firm, white	Medium
Mussels (farmed)	Delicate, off-white	Full

THE BEST CATCH

Fish	Texture, Color	Flavor
Oysters (farmed)	Delicate, off-white	Full
Sablefish/black cod	Firm, white	Medium, oily
Salmon (wild)	Firm, red	Full, semi-oily
Sardines	Medium, off-white	Full, oily
Scallops*	Delicate, white	Mild
Shrimp* (U.S.)	Medium, white	Mild
Sole*	Delicate, white	Mild
Squid*	Firm	Mild
Striped bass	Firm, white	Mild
Sturgeon (farmed)	Firm, white	Medium, oily
Swordfish (Pacific)	Firm, white	Full, semi-oily
Tilapia	Medium, white	Mild
Rainbow trout	Medium, white	Medium
Tuna: albacore, bigeye, yellowfin (longline*)	Firm, dark	Full
White sea bass	Firm, off-white	Mild

(* Indicates acceptable alternatives that aren't yet on the Avoid list, but may be headed there.)

Throw It Back

Whether the population is overfished, the method of fishing produces an abundance of bycatch, or the species is exposed to high levels of toxins or mercury, the following seafood is on the Avoid list. Smart alternatives are included, as well. Can't resist sea bass or snapper? Just don't make a habit of it. Eating a variety of different fish, even if one is on the Avoid list, is a good way to keep from eating too much of one of the no-nos.

JUST SAY NAH

Instead of:	Try:	Texture/Color/Flavor
Chilean sea bass	Mahi mahi	Firm/white/medium
Cod (Atlantic)	Pacific cod, hoki	Delicate/white/mild
Flounder (Atlantic)	Skate	Firm/white/mild
Grouper	Striped bass	Firm/white/mild
Halibut (Atlantic)	Pacific halibut	Firm/white/mild
Monkfish	Yellowtail tuna	Firm/dark/full
Orange roughy	Catfish, tilapia	Medium/white/mild
Rockfish	Pacific ocean perch	Medium/pink/medium
Salmon (farmed, Atlantic)	Pacific, Alaskan, or wild salmon; Arctic char	Firm/red/full
Shark	Pacific halibut	Firm/medium
Shrimp (imported, trawled)	U.S./Gulf Shrimp	Medium/white/mild
Red snapper	Sea bream	Firm/white/mild
Sole (Atlantic)	Striped bass	Firm/white/mild
Sturgeon (wild)	Sturgeon (farmed)	Firm/white/medium
Swordfish (Atlantic, imported)	Pacific swordfish	Firm/white/full
Bluefin tuna	Ahi/yellowtail tuna	Firm/dark/full

Most of the Chilean sea bass served in restaurants isn't sea bass, much less from Chile. The firm, white fish is actually Patagonian toothfish, a species on the verge of extinction. Because the fish is caught in international waters, regulating the catch is difficult. Many restaurants have joined the "Take a pass on Chilean Sea Bass" campaign and removed it from their menus.

WILD VS. FARMED

Another fishy issue: Whether fish and seafood are better caught in the wild or farmed. The consensus is that wild is better, particularly salmon, because of the pollution produced by coastline farming. Farm-raised oysters, clams, and mussels are the exception because they actually filter and clean the water they're raised in. The ideal catch is farmed inland because it does not contaminate the ocean or infiltrate the species of wild fish. Trout, tilapia, and catfish are common inland-farmed fish and several companies have figured out how to raise shrimp in self-contained, inland freshwater ponds.

LAGNIAPPE

Swordfish, shark, king mackerel, and tuna—the big carnivores of the sea—are more likely to contain high levels of mercury and other toxins because they're not only exposed to the bad stuff, they also eat smaller fish that contain it. Smaller fish and seafood that live on plants, like oysters, scallops, shrimp, and lobster, have the lowest toxin levels.

CAVIAR 101

The soft, oozy pop of caviar on the tongue is a divine sensation for some, but not all. That two tablespoons of fish eggs could set you back as much as $200 in a restaurant is probably the bigger hurdle for most people. If you've ever wanted to order it but don't know how or wondered what's so special about the salty larvae, these FAQs will clear things up.

Why is caviar so pricey? Two reasons: (1) The legendary fish eggs from the Caspian and Black Seas come from sturgeon, an endangered species whose population has been decimated by industrialization, poaching, and shady black market trading. Low supply + high demand = $$$. (2) To produce high-grade caviar, it must be washed, salted, and cold-cured, a process so meticulous that it's usually done by hand to keep the delicate eggs from being crushed. This kind of manual labor doesn't come cheap.

What are the different types of caviar? In Europe, only sturgeon roe from the Caspian can be called caviar, and each type of caviar is named for the species of sturgeon it comes from. Fish eggs from any other fish are called roe. **Beluga**, the most expensive, has the biggest "berries" (which is what you should call the eggs if you want to sound like a veteran caviar eater). Belugas swim the northern, colder waters of the Caspian and produce grey to grey-black caviar that melts on your tongue. **Osetra**, a medium-size yellow to brown caviar, comes from the southern part of the Caspian and has a silky texture and nutty flavor. **Sevruga**, the least expensive and lightest gray caviar, has the smallest, most intensely flavored and firm berries of the Caspian sturgeon. The firm **sterlet**, a small, golden-colored caviar, is all but extinct and extremely rare.

Beluga caviar is graded by its size and color. "0" denotes the darkest berries, "00" are medium-dark, and "000" are the lightest. Purists say 0s are the best. Berry color depends on what the fish eats, water temperature, and other environmental factors. If you see the word *malossol* (Russian for "lightly salted") on the caviar tin or menu, it's a notch above the rest. All caviar is salted, but the more subtle the salt, the better the caviar.

TALES OF THE FEAST

Russia and Iran, countries that surround the Caspian Sea, are the major exporters of caviar today, but in the late 1800s most of the world's caviar came from American sturgeon that filled the Great Lakes and the Hudson River. In New York, caviar earned the nickname "Albany beef" because it was so abundant. Saloons served it as a bar snack, and customers dropped it into their beers to make "Albany beer."

What is the best season for caviar? Restaurants that specialize in full caviar service, like Petrossian and Caviar Russe in New York City and Aureole in Las Vegas and New York, serve it year-round with the help of careful packing and freezing. However, the best seasons to splurge on caviar are fall and spring, when fish are spawning.

Do I have to sell a kidney to afford it? Not necessarily. American "caviar" is about half as expensive as imported. Because Caspian sturgeon are hovering near extinction and the United States periodically bans importing beluga and osetra in last-ditch attempts at preservation, producers in the U.S. have stepped in to fill the void with the roe of white and hackleback sturgeon, paddlefish (a close cousin of sturgeon), bowfin (also called choupique), salmon, whitefish, and trout. Be aware that restaurants and retailers in the U.S. aren't bound by the European definition of the word caviar, so the salted, cured roe of any fish can be called caviar. However, unless the caviar comes from a species of sturgeon, menus should list the name of the fish variety, such as paddlefish caviar.

How do I eat it? Because these fragile eggs are prone to picking up tinny flavors from metal, caviar is served in a glass or mother-of-pearl dish set over a bed of ice with a teeny spoon for scooping. A formal caviar service is traditionally served with small buckwheat pancakes called blini (BLEE-nee) or buttered toast points, and garnishes like crème fraîche (crehm FRESH), lemon, capers, boiled egg, and onion. The sipper of choice for caviar is an iced Russian vodka or brut Champagne.

"The caviar connoisseur might notice a slight difference in American farm-raised white sturgeon berries, which are slightly larger than Caspian. But for the average person, there is no difference other than price."
—EVERALD TOMLINSON, caviar consultant,
Petrossian, New York City

Spawned in the U.S.A.

White and **hackleback sturgeon** caviar has small, smooth berries like beluga, but is similar to osetra in its sweet, earthy nuttiness. Like sevruga, the medium, pearly gray berries from **paddlefish** pack a briny, ocean flavor. American Golden caviar, from the tiny, yellow-gold **whitefish** roe, has a slight crunch. Plump, orange **salmon** roe is juicy, salty, and mildly fishy. **Choupique** roe is naturally black, which makes it look like most sturgeon roe, but it has a distinct, tangy flavor of its own. **Trout** roe is medium in size, slightly sticky, and translucent.

OYSTERS: POETRY IN OCEAN

Either you love raw oysters or you're afraid of them. If you fall into the former category, a well-shucked platter at the beginning of your meal, with a martini or a glass of Champagne or Sancerre, is the ultimate luxury—and a signal to your waiter that you're a serious eater and, more important, not squeamish. Even if you're reluctant to try something so squishy and strange, it's never too late to ease into the habit. When you're feeling brave, start with small, creamy, and mild oysters that won't shock your system, like Kumamotos.

The most important information to know about oysters is where they come from. The tumultuous waters that East Coast oysters call home tend to make the meat lean, but more briny and assertive compared to the creamy, plump, and sweet West Coast oysters that live in colder but gentler waters. Warm-water Gulf Coast oysters are usually meaty and less flavorful, and best suited for cooking.

Raw oysters are served in restaurants year-round, but during the summer months opt for varieties from Canada, the Northeast, and the Pacific Northwest, where water temperatures stay cool all year. Mid-Atlantic and Gulf oysters (think Virginia, Louisiana) are better in the months that end in *r*—September, October, November, December.

On the Plate

Oysters on the half shell are pried open with special knives and the muscle connected to the shell is severed. The oysters are served in the "half shell" over a bed of chipped ice with small cocktail forks. Expert shuckers in restaurants try to reserve the juice inside the shells so you literally get a taste of the ocean when you gobble down the contents. Classic garnishes include wedges of lemon, cocktail sauce, and French mignonette, a chilled mixture of diced shallots, vinegar, and pepper.

Oysters Rockefeller is a classic appetizer of oysters baked with a spinach-bacon mixture on top.

To slurp, or not to slurp? It's not unusual to see people pour oysters directly from the shell into their mouths in restaurants. If you want to be prim and proper about it: Spritz the oyster with lemon or dab it with sauce using your cocktail fork. Hold the shell in your left hand and, with the oyster fork in your right, lift the oyster from the shell and eat it in one bite.

"Most people slide oysters into their mouths to get all of the juice. That's how I eat them. No lemon. Just a little bit of fresh ground black pepper the way the French do."
—JACK LAMB, owner, Jack's Luxury Oyster Bar, New York

Vocabulary for the Oyster Connoisseur

Oyster eaters like their insider lingo almost as much as wine drinkers. Familiarize yourself with this short glossary of words if you want to understand the menu or the waiter's descriptions about these tasty bivalves.

Briny means it tastes like the ocean—salty and vaguely fishy, but not in a bad way.

Creamy oysters have a smooth and rich mouthfeel, which makes the flavor and texture linger in your mouth longer.

Crisp or **clean** oysters have an edgier mouthfeel, so the flavor is more tight and doesn't cling the way creamy oysters do.

Cucumber flavors are very subtle and perfumey.

Melon is vaguely sweet and fruity.

Metallic and **flinty** notes are sharp and make your mouth water.

Salty is like briny, but without the fish flavor.

Sweet oysters aren't sugary; they're unsalty or lack brininess.

BE A BUFF

Field Guide to Meat, by Aliza Green; *The Complete Meat Cookbook,* by Bruce Aidells and Denis Kelly; *Fish and Shellfish,* by James Peterson; *National Audubon Society Seafood Lover's Almanac; Consider the Oyster,* by M. F. K. Fisher; *The Joy of Oysters,* by Lori McKean; *Caviar: The Strange History and Uncertain Future of the World's Most Coveted Delicacy,* by Inga Saffron

7

SEASON'S EATING

thinking **GLOBALLY,** *eating* **LOCALLY**

At average restaurants, the produce that shows up on your plate with an entrée usually seems like an afterthought—an obligatory steamed, limp sidekick overshadowed by the main character of the meal. Not so in the realm of chic eats. Thanks to nouvelle cuisine, restaurant veg-olutionaries like Chez Panisse chef Alice Waters, and the hard work of local farmers, farmer's markets, and organizations like Slow Food, fancy restaurants are giving much more of the spotlight to locally grown, seasonal, and heirloom fruits and veggies. It's become commonplace for chefs to showcase farmer's market picks on seasonal menus and for waiters to wax poetic about the organic farms that supply the restaurant's white asparagus or heirloom beans.

If you're not accustomed to eating posh produce or thinking about how it was grown or what's in season because everything from apples to zucchini is available year-round, this extra information can make deciding what to eat even more intimidating. When you're considering the night's specials and wondering what kohlrabi is or whether you'll like spaghetti squash, the thing to keep in mind is how it ended up on the menu. Chefs at upscale restaurants pick and choose what to serve based on what's fresh, in season, and grown with care. Even if you think mashed potatoes and spinach might be better with your entrée, you should trust that the chef— who knows the farmers, gets first crack at limited supplies of rare, specialty produce, tastes everything, and turns away anything that isn't up to standards—knows best. When you see fiddlehead ferns and ramps on the menu, it's because the restaurant was able to score these unusual items during the short two or three weeks they were available. When you don't see carrots, tomatoes, or asparagus on the menu even though you see them all year in the grocery store, it's because the chef won't sacrifice quality and taste for the sake of serving what's familiar but flavorless out of season. If you have a little faith and are willing to take risks, ordering the exotic, local, and in-season produce restaurants offer, you won't be disappointed.

What's in it for you? Flavor. Unlike industrial produce that has been genetically engineered to have an unnaturally long shelf life and to withstand heat, cold, bugs, and cross-country/cross-continent shipping, seasonal, local fruits and vegetables are prone to bumps and bruises and are short-lived, but they are unmatched in flavor and texture. If you've ever cut into a mealy, pink tomato in December or eaten a bland strawberry in October, you know the difference. By creating menus based on what's in season, chefs are limited in what they can serve, but the upside is that you get to eat produce at the very peak of perfection. Of course, that means you won't have pears in June or sweet corn in January, but after all, Mother Nature didn't intend it. Even if some restaurants can afford to buy off-season peppers from Mexico or kiwis from New Zealand, the food doesn't have the same appeal—or flavor—as Queen Anne cherries or pattypan squash from the teeny farm two counties over.

Getting Fresh: Spotting Seasonal and Green Menus

How will you know if you're eating in-season or greenhouse pea shoots, or industrially grown tomatoes? Restaurants will not pass up an opportunity to showcase elite produce, particularly if it's a peak-season specialty. The following are signs the restaurant is serving seasonal, local, or farmer's market produce.

- **The menu changes regularly.** If the menu cycles with the seasons, whether it's a weekly tweaking of ingredients and specials or a complete menu turnover every two or three months, the chef is constantly making decisions about what to serve based on what's fresh and available. If you don't know, ask your waiter how often the menu changes or look for featured, in-season ingredients on the menu.

- **The restaurant brags about where the food comes from.** It's not impolite to ask "Does the chef buy from the farmer's market?" or "Are these mushrooms grown locally?" or "Where did this divine artichoke come from?" The waiter may have to ask the kitchen for details, but green cuisine restaurants will be able to answer these questions, no problem.

"Judge a restaurant by its ability to tell you where your food comes from. For what you're paying for the meal, you deserve to know and it's fair game to ask whether something is organic, or from a local farm, or in season. Chefs appreciate diners who care about this information, because at this level of restaurant, the chefs care a lot."
—PATRICK MARTINS, cofounder of Heritage Foods USA

- **The menu reads like a farmer's market tour guide.** If it identifies local farms by name, as in "Harmony Valley Farm baby carrots," or lists specific vegetable or fruit varieties, like Silver Queen white corn or Emerald Beaut plums, the restaurant is clearly making an effort to serve local, seasonal foods.

MARKET TO MENU

You may see some of these buzzwords for better food on menus in green cuisine restaurants.

Heirloom fruits, vegetables, and beans are older varieties of native, nonhybrid plants grown by open pollination (which means seeds are saved and replanted). Crop after crop, year after year, the plant stays true to type in flavor, color, and size. Heirlooms are more susceptible to pests and genetic quirks, so they may be less "attractive" (think: funky shapes or spots) and have a shorter shelf life, but the payoff is in their unique, full flavors.

Organic fruits and vegetables come from USDA-certified farms and are grown and processed without the use of fertilizers, insecticides, additives, or artificial coloring and flavoring, as outlined by the 1990 Federal Organic Foods Protection Act.

Local (or locally grown) is an unregulated word that indicates the food is grown or produced in the vicinity of where you're eating it. Because there aren't any regulations defining the word, the food may be from the chef's own vegetable garden or a farm three hundred miles away.

Sustainable isn't a word likely to pop up on a menu and it doesn't have a legal definition. Relative to food production, it's a philosophy that promotes low-impact, renewable, quality food production with no side effects, such as pollution, waste, or poor working conditions.

Brand names on the menu are a good thing. When you see the name of a farm or a ranch (Blue Valley Farms mushrooms or Snake River Farms Kobe beef), or a specific species of fruit or vegetable (Black Mission figs or Taxi tomatoes), the restaurant is showing off the food's pedigree.

Beware of the warm, fuzzy pitch. With the growing awareness and interest in green cuisine, some restaurants are jumping on the bandwagon in word alone. Waiters gush about hand-filleted fish (uh, how *else* is it filleted?) and menus hijack the names of farms and buzzwords like *organic* or *heirloom* to justify hiking up their prices, but they don't practice what they preach. Be savvy to overhyped menu descriptions, do some research, and keep an eye out for the fakes.

Eat Your Vegetables: Peak Seasons for the Plants on Your Plate

Because there are no limits to how chefs prepare vegetables, the most important things you need to know are the best seasons for your favorites and the flavors and foods they go well with.

Of course, growing seasons and the availability of seasonal produce vary from region to region. The following chart reflects the season when veggies are at their prime wherever they're grown, whether it's asparagus from northern California in April or sweet potatoes from Texas in October.

PLANT FOOD		
Vegetable	Season	Food Friends
Artichokes	Spring/summer/fall	Butter, olive oil, vinaigrette, Hollandaise sauce
Arugula (a.k.a. rocket)	Year-round, greenhouse	Vinaigrette, beets, goat cheese, mozzarella, nuts, olives

PLANT FOOD

Vegetable	Season	Food Friends
Asparagus	Spring	Butter, Parmesan cheese, velouté sauce, Hollandaise sauce, vinaigrette
Avocado	Winter/spring	Cilantro, crab, grapefruit, lime, shrimp, tomato
Beets	Summer/fall	Goat cheese, potatoes, beef
Bok choy	Summer/fall/winter	Shiitake mushrooms, soy sauce, seafood, beef
Broccoli	Fall/winter/spring	Butter, lemon, balsamic vinegar, chicken
Brussels sprouts	Fall/winter/spring	Butter, shallots, bacon
Cabbage	Year-round	Butter, onion, potato, sausage, game birds
Carrots	Fall/winter/spring	Celery, most herbs, shallots, cinnamon, chicken, beef
Cauliflower	Fall/winter	Butter, cream, garlic, lemon, thyme
Celery	Summer/fall/winter	Blue and Gruyère cheese, soup, fish
Chard	Summer/fall	Olive oil, lemon, garlic, vinegar, olives, cured meats
Corn	Summer/fall	Butter, red onion, basil, tarragon, shellfish
Cucumber	Spring/summer/fall	Buttermilk, yogurt, chervil, chives, mint, scallions, salmon
Eggplant	Summer/fall	Tomato, mutton, white meat
Endive	Summer/fall	Vinaigrette, cured black olives, bacon
Fava beans	Spring/summer	Chiles, cilantro, garlic, onions, oregano, fish, poultry
Fennel	Summer/fall	Olive oil, citrus, chicken, shellfish

PLANT FOOD

Vegetable	Season	Food Friends
Green beans	Summer	Butter, olive oil, dill, lemon, marjoram, almonds
Greens (beet, collard, dandelion, mustard)	Year-round	Aged hard cheese, vinegar, lemon, onion, bacon
Kale	Winter/spring	Bacon fat, lemon, onion, smoked meat, sausage
Mushrooms	Year-round	Cream, onion, pasta, fish, chicken, beef
Okra	Spring/summer/fall	Vinegar, lemon, tomato, onion, rice, corn
Parsnips	Fall/winter	Cream, apples, brown sugar, other root vegetables, soup, stew, ragout
Peas	Spring/summer/fall	Artichokes, chives, mint, salmon, scallops, shrimp
Peppers (bell)	Summer/fall	Garlic, chiles, onion, pork, sausage, poultry, beef
Potatoes	Year-round	Butter, olive oil, vinaigrette, onion, pork, chicken
Rhubarb	Spring/summer	Brown sugar, ginger, berries, duck, oily fish
Rutabaga	Fall/winter/spring	Cream, lemon, marjoram, onion, thyme, duck, pork, lamb
Salad greens	Year-round	Vinaigrette, lemon, cucumber, tomato, anchovies
Snow and snap peas	Spring/summer	Artichokes, chives, mint, tarragon, sorrel, seafood
Sorrel	Spring	Salads, fish, veal
Spinach	Year-round	Aged cheese, sour cream, nutmeg, garlic, onion, mushrooms

PLANT FOOD		
Vegetable	Season	Food Friends
Squash blossoms	Summer/fall	Olive oil, goat cheese, tomato
Squash (zucchini, pattypan, yellow)	Summer	Olive oil, goat cheese, feta, garlic, marjoram, mint, onion, oregano, pasta
Squash, winter (buttercup, Cuban, acorn, spaghetti, pumpkin)	Summer/fall/winter	Butter, olive oil, honey, garlic, onion, rosemary, sage, pasta, lamb
Sweet potatoes	Fall/winter/spring	Butter, brown sugar, honey, ginger, pecans, rum, bourbon
Tomatoes	Summer	Feta, mozzarella, cucumber, salad greens, mint, oregano, pasta, shellfish, veal

LAGNIAPPE

Artichokes contain a compound called cynarin that can make other food and wine taste sweet; the same component in asparagus turns wine bitter and metallic. Consult your sommelier before you order a $100 Cabernet Sauvignon if your meal involves either vegetable.

Not Your Garden Variety:
Freaky Veggies Restaurants Love to Serve

Vegetables provide a great medium for experimenting with flavors and textures, and it's likely you'll see some exotic produce you've never heard of or eaten in the more high-falutin' restaurants. Some of us may shy away from the funkier stuff—and, hey, when you're eating fifty bucks in food, who can blame you? The truth is, restaurants are the best place to push your limits because these rare, hybrid, and strange vegetables morph into exquisite dishes in the hands of a professional chef. But first, you need a general idea of what you're ordering.

Broccoflower is a cross between broccoli and cauliflower. It has a tight bunch of light green florets clustered onto a cauliflower-like head.

Broccolini is a new crossbreed of broccoli and Chinese kale that sometimes goes by the trademarked name Asparation. It has long, thin stems tipped with small florets.

Broccoli rabe is a long, thin-stalked Italian broccoli with a few florets, a.k.a. **rapini.**

Cardoons are a relative of the artichoke that looks like a loose bunch of celery. They are served fried and au gratin.

Celeriac (seh-LER-ee-ak), a.k.a. celery root or knob celery, is the knotty, bulbous root of celery. Its light celery flavor makes it suitable for eating raw in salads, but it is also cooked—usually boiled and pureed into mashed potatoes.

Chayote (chi-OH-tay), or mirliton, is a light-green vegetable with a flavor and texture somewhere between an apple and a cucumber. It can be eaten raw in salads, baked, steamed and used in stuffing, or sliced and sautéed.

Fiddleheads are the green, curled stems of any young fern, with a flavor that's a cross between asparagus and artichoke. They are available from April to July in various locales, but have an extremely short season (about two weeks) before the stems unfurl and turn bitter.

Haricot vert (ah-ree-koh VEHR) is a fancy way of saying "green string bean," and usually refers to the slender French variety.

Jicama (HEE-kah-mah) is a crisp, white vegetable with the texture of a potato when cooked in soups or stews or tossed into sautés; it has the crunch of celery when raw, usually in salads.

Kohlrabi (kohl-RAH-bee), or cabbage turnip, is a multipurpose vegetable used for its greens, similar to beet or turnip greens, and its root, which is firm and crisp with a sweet-hot radish flavor.

Lotus root is the starchy, crisp stem of a water lily. A series of seed tunnels run through the root, which makes for ornate crosscuts that can be fried and eaten plain or added to salads, stir-fries, or soups.

Nopales (noh-PAH-lays) are cactus leaves without the prickly parts and can be grilled, boiled, marinated, or sautéed. They have a chewy texture and a mildly tart, green-vegetable flavor.

Ramps are small, intensely flavored wild leeks that are usually sautéed or fried, but can also be eaten raw (like chives). Because they are rare and picked in the wild, they are available only in farmer's markets in short spurts between March and July.

Salsify is a dark-skinned white root vegetable that can be roasted, like other root vegetables, or baked.

FIELDS OF GREENS

If iceberg wedges and piles of romaine are the full extent of your lettuce repertoire, you may not recognize the squiggly and peppery greens that show up in snazzy restaurant salads. Tasty, crisp field greens come in all shapes and sizes, and because they can be grown year-round in greenhouses are standard on many menus. Some are faintly bitter (chicory, curly endive, radicchio, dandelion), some are peppery (arugula, watercress, radish sprouts), some are tart (purslane, sorrel), and others are mild and sweet (lamb's tongue, oak leaf, baby spinach, escarole). **Mesclun** is a classic mix of the shoots and leaves of young field greens with different colors and textures, usually chicory, endive, dandelion, arugula, lamb's lettuce, and oak leaf.

EAT THIS

The word *avocado* comes from the Aztec word *ahuacatl,* which means "testicle"—a not-so-subtle reference to the shape of the fruit and the way it hangs in pairs from trees.

Unforbidden Fruits: Peak Seasons for Mother Nature's Candy

The sweet stuff isn't just for dessert anymore. Although fresh fruit will most likely show up in pies, crisps, sorbets, and other treats at the end of the meal, chefs also use the sweet, tart, and tangy edibles in the raw or in stewed fruit compotes, purees, and sauces as a flavor contrast for savory entrées. As with veggies, fruit growing seasons and availability vary greatly from region to region. The following chart reflects the peak season for the fruit where it is grown best. An easy tip to remember: Delicate, thin-skinned fruits, such as berries, cherries, peaches, and nectarines, are best in the spring and summer, and hearty, thick-skinned fruits, such as apples, oranges, pears, persimmon, and grapefruit, are fall/winter favorites.

NATURE'S NECTAR

Fruit	Season
Apple	Fall/winter
Avocado	Winter/spring
Banana	Year-round
Blackberry	Summer
Blueberry	Spring/summer
Cherry	Summer
Cranberry	Fall
Fig	Summer/fall
Grape	Year-round
Grapefruit	Year-round
Guava	Spring/summer
Kiwi	Fall/winter/spring
Lemon	Spring/summer
Lime	Spring/summer
Lychee	Summer
Mango	Spring/summer
Melon	Summer/fall
Nectarine	Spring/summer
Orange	Fall/winter/spring
Papaya	Spring/summer
Passionfruit	Summer/fall
Peach	Spring/summer
Pear	Fall/winter/spring
Persimmon	Fall/winter
Pineapple	Spring/summer
Plum	Summer/fall
Pomegranate	Fall
Pomelo	Winter
Quince	Fall/winter
Raspberry	Summer
Strawberry	Spring/summer
Tangerine	Winter/early spring
Watermelon	Summer

LAGNIAPPE

If you suffer from indigestion on a regular basis or after big, rich meals, eat papaya or chew a few papaya pills (available at most drugstores). Papain, an enzyme found in the fruit, aids digestion. It's also a popular meat tenderizer.

Herbs and Aromatics:
Knowing Herbes de Provence from Bouquet Garni

A quick lesson: Herbs are the fresh or dried stems and leaves of certain plants. Spices are fresh or dried flowers, fruit, seeds, bark, and root. The pulverized, dust-flavored herbs and spices in your pantry bear little resemblance to the pungent dried and fresh aromatics used in restaurants. As with produce, chefs can get their hands on the best, most fragrant goods money can buy, and they aren't afraid to use them. Typically, when an herb or a spice is a major player in a dish, it will show up in the menu description. Whether the cuisine is traditional or ethnic, the aromatics familiar or foreign, don't shy away from a dish with an unusual or lengthy list of seasonings. This is why you're paying big bucks to eat. Those little bits of flavor give depth and definition to food you can't re-create at home. The culinary panoply on menus is also part of the fancy restaurant pretense. Impressing you with exotic and quirky ingredients is a restaurant's clever way of making a dish sound sexy and extravagant, which makes it easier to charge a small fortune for what might otherwise be called "chicken in herbs and spices."

EAT THIS

In Japanese cuisine, herbs and spices are practically nonexistent. Garlic, ginger, and chile peppers are used sparingly, but the food is typically au naturel. Chefs prefer to let the natural flavors of the ingredients shine through, without all of the extra seasoning.

CLASSIC HERB COMBOS

Herbes de provence, a mixture of fresh or dried thyme, rosemary, fennel seed, lavender, marjoram, bay leaf, basil, sage, and savory, is often used on grilled foods. **Fines herbes** is a combination of chopped herbs, traditionally parsley, chervil, tarragon, and chives, used to season meat, sauces, butter, sautéed vegetables, and egg dishes. **Bouquet garni**, a bundle of herbs added to sauces or stocks for flavoring, contains parsley, thyme, and bay leaves, but Italian chefs may add sage and rosemary. **Quatre epices**, or four spices, is a mixture of white pepper, nutmeg, ginger or cinnamon, and cloves used on roasts, poultry, and winter root vegetables and in desserts. **Curry powder** is a blend of ground spices including cumin, coriander, fenugreek seeds, turmeric, black pepper, red pepper, cinnamon, ginger, cardamom, nutmeg, allspice, garlic, dill, and celery seeds. **Garam masala**, an Indian spice mix, contains cinnamon, bay, cumin, coriander, cardamom, peppercorns, cloves, and mace. **Dukka** is a blend of sesame seeds, roasted chickpeas, coriander, cumin, and mint used in traditional Egyptian dishes. **Chinese five-spice powder** is a blend of Szechuan peppercorns, cinnamon, cloves, star anise, and fennel.

BE A BUFF

www.sustainabletable.org; www.chefscollaborative.org; *Eat Here*, by Brian Halweil; *Field Guide to Produce*, by Aliza Green; *The Contemporary Encyclopedia of Herbs and Spices*, by Tony Hill

8

SAY *FROMAGE*

a fine **DINER'S** *grand* **FINALE:** *the* **CHEESE COURSE**

Good-bye, cheese and crackers. Hello, Camembert and raisin-walnut bread. At last, the cheese course—a quintessential tradition in European fine dining—is finding its way to fine American restaurants. Many diners are embracing *le fromage* with the same kind of feverish enthusiasm that wine lovers display for *terroir,* and the pursuit of the finer cheeses in life has become a bona fide foodist movement.

But with the love of cheese, as with wine, come questions. If they're both blue cheeses, what's the difference between Gorgonzola and Roquefort? Can one wine go with five distinctly different cheeses? What happens if you don't recognize any names on a huge cheese menu? And are you really supposed to eat the rind? Because the cheese course is still a relatively new addition to American menus, it's hard for many of us to wrap our heads around the idea of ending a gut-busting seven-course meal with a round of cheese, as the French do, or even starting a fancy dinner with such heavy, fatty fare when the entrée is still to come. This chapter is devised to help you get over that hump. You'll learn enough about how cheese is made to spot the different styles, figure out what your favorites are, select a well-balanced board, and pair your choices with wine—skills you can use in a restaurant or at home. When it's all over with, you'll understand why cheese is not only an outstanding addition to almost any multicourse food orgy but also a meal in itself.

How to Say "Cheese" in Five Languages

Fromage [froh-MAHZH] - French
Queso [KEH-soh] - Spanish
Formaggio [fohr-MAH-joh] - Italian
Käse [KAY-zeh] - German
Chizu [CHEE-zoo] - Japanese

TALES OF THE FEAST

The Italian and French words for cheese, *formaggio* and *fromage*, come from the Greek word *formos*, which was a wicker basket used to hold the curdled milk as it formed into cheese. Although France gets the lion's share of the credit for turning cheese making into an art form, the earliest evidence of cheese production dates back to 3000 B.C. in Mesopotamia, or modern-day Iraq.

Got Lactose? The Milk That Makes the Cheese

Most cheese is made from cow's, goat's, or sheep's milk. Cheese menus, names, and labels often list the milk animal, so it's helpful to know the word for each animal in French, Spanish, and Italian, and just for kicks, Latin.

MILK IT				
English	French	Spanish	Italian	Latin
Cow	*vache*	*vaca*	*mucca*	*vacca*
Goat	*chèvre*	*cabra*	*capra*	*capra*
Sheep	*brebis*	*oveja*	*pecora*	*ovis*

EAT THIS

It takes about ten pounds of milk to make one pound of cheese.

"Sheep's milk cheeses will always be my favorite because they're so high in butterfat. They're very, very rich."
—BARRY KING, 2005 executive director,
American Cheese Society

CHEESE: WANTED DEAD OR ALIVE

No serious discussion of eating cheese can take place without mentioning the issue of pasteurization. Although the tastiest cheeses tend to be made from fresh, raw milk, U.S. Food and Drug Administration guidelines outlaw importing or selling raw-milk cheeses aged less than sixty days. The law doesn't affect hard raw-milk cheeses like Cheddar, Parmigiano-Reggiano, and Gruyère, which are aged four to six months, but it's the reason you won't taste the best Brie, Camembert, or Crottin de Chavignol (that's goat cheese, to you) the French have to offer unless you go to Europe. To be sold in the United States, the milk of these young, soft cheeses must be pasteurized—heated to a certain temperature to kill bacteria. Anyone who has eaten true French Camembert and tasted what passes for it in this country can attest to the difference between raw- and pasteurized-milk cheeses. Pasteurization is to cheese what microwaving is to filet mignon. It gets the job done faster and more cheaply, but food loses depth, flavor, and texture—its identity—in the process. In the best raw-milk cheeses, if you've got the 'buds for it, you can taste hints of the region where the animal grazed and pick up notes of clover, herbs, wildflowers, and other grasses. Serious cheesers say heating milk cooks the distinct regional character out of a cheese.

"Unpasteurized cheeses are alive, and living cheeses are not only tastier and more aromatic, they also have a much longer shelf life."
—MAX MCCALMAN, maître fromager, Artisanal, New York City, author of *The Cheese Plate*

From Milk to Mold to Mmmm: How Cheese Is Made (in 500 Words or Less)

All cheese starts with a batch of milk. For large-scale production, milk is pooled from different dairy farms. Artisanal cheese makers who produce smaller lots use milk collected from local farms or a single farm. Once the milk is pooled it is pasteurized (or not, if it is used in a raw-milk cheese aged over sixty days), and a starter culture containing bacteria such as *Streptococci* or *Lactobacilli* is added. The starter reacts with the lactose in milk, turning it into lactic acid, which enables milk proteins to coagulate and form curds when rennet is added. Once rennet is mixed in, the temperature of the milk is tweaked according to the type of cheese being made. It takes anywhere from thirty minutes to two hours for the milk to gel and set. At this point, the liquid formerly known as milk is solid enough to cut into fine, medium, or coarse curds, depending on the variety of cheese.

Next, whey is extracted from the curd. The simplest way to understand this part is to think of a curd as a jellylike sponge. If it's a small sponge, or curd, there's less room to hold liquid (in this case, whey). A bigger sponge, or curd, will hold more liquid. Small, fine curds will produce a hard, dry cheese, like Cheddar; large, coarse curds result in softer cheeses, like mozzarella and Brie.

Once the curds are cut, they are pressed, cooked, salted, milled, shaken, stretched, and spun—just a few of many methods for extracting whey and treating curds—depending on the cheese. For example, fine curds for Cheddar are scalded in hot water, then milled (a process called "cheddaring," which involves repeatedly cutting and stacking curds to expel whey). Then the curds are ground into itty-bitty pieces, salted, and pressed into huge molds. To make hard, aged cheeses like Parmigiano-Reggiano, curds are cooked and pressed. Mozzarella curds are dunked into vats of boiling-hot water, and the glob of curd that sinks and blends at the bottom of the tub is stretched and pulled and formed into balls of the soft cheese.

Last, the curds are salted, which kick-starts the starter culture and controls how a cheese ripens. Salt is added in one of four ways: It can be mixed directly into the curds, the curds may be bathed in salt water, or the surface of the cheese may be rubbed with salt or swabbed with a brine-soaked cloth. Once the cheese is formed or pressed into a mold, it's ready for ripening. As they age, some cheeses are washed with liquids like beer or wine, and others are rotated and flipped so the milk's butterfat spreads evenly throughout the cheese. Blue-veined cheeses are pierced with needles after salting, and bacteria grow to form a green-blue paste where the oxygen seeps in. The end result: In humidity- and temperature-controlled storage rooms, the lowly curd transforms into cheese as bacteria from the starter culture do what Mother Nature intended.

Sacre bleu! According to cheese legend, the bacteria in the starter culture for Roquefort cheese, *Penicillium roqueforti*, was discovered after a sheepherder abandoned his lunch—a loaf of rye bread and cheese curds—in a cave. Spores from the moldy rye bread mingled with the curds and the famously sharp, salty sheep's milk cheese was born.

Cheese-Spotting: How Cheese Is Classified

All cheese starts out the same—as milk—but the different methods used to make cheese produce very different results: It can be sharp and crumbly, creamy and oozing, semisoft, stinky, and countless other variations. Along with the type of milk (cow, goat, sheep), cheeses are categorized primarily by their texture and appearance (not flavor) into roughly eight different classes. A cheese can fit into more than one category, but once you get the gist of the different classifications, you'll know how to select a diverse cheese course that represents the different milks, styles, textures, and flavors of cheese.

Fresh cheeses, like chèvre (goat cheese), cottage cheese, ricotta, and fromage blanc, are uncooked and, for the most part, unripened (not aged) curd. Some types, including cream cheese, ricotta, and feta, are drained so that more whey (liquid) is released. Others, like Robiola and creamy, sweet mascarpone, are not drained.

Soft-ripened cheeses are also called **bloomy** because they ripen from the outside in, resulting in a thin, white, peach-fuzzy rind encasing the soft, sometimes oozy cheese. Examples include Brie, Camembert, Saint André, Explorateur, Gratte-Paille, Brillat-Savarin, and Gaperon.

Washed-rind, semisoft cheeses like Taleggio, Robiola Lombardia, Epoisses, Pont-L'Eveque, Mahon, Gorgonzola, Reblochon, and Livarot are rubbed or bathed with salt water, beer, wine, grape must, and other liquids to encourage an exterior mold that makes the cheese ripen from the rind inward.

Waxed-rind, semisoft cheeses are dipped into an inedible wax and tend to be smooth and mild, like fontina, Bel Paese, Gouda, and Edam.

Natural and **brushed-rind** cheeses have little or no rind, and with the exception of light, fresh chèvres, are dense and usually aged longer than other cheeses. This group includes Stilton, Comté, Gruyère, Emmental, Manchego, Romano, and Parmigiano-Reggiano.

Blue-veined, piquant cheeses like Maytag, Roquefort, Gorgonzola, Cabrales, and Stilton are pretty easy to spot because of the green, blue, and sometimes purplish marbling that runs through the interior.

Uncooked, pressed cheeses are made from unheated curd that has been pressed to expel as much whey as possible, so they are firm, like Cheddar, Manchego, Morbier, and pecorino Romano.

Cooked, pressed cheeses, such as Gouda, Cantal, Gruyère, Parmigiano-Reggiano, Appenzeller, Emmental, and Boerenkaas, are made by heating and pressing the curds to expel whey, which makes them hard.

Cheese Words You Need to Know

Affinage: The slow and delicate process of refining an artisanal cheese, including washing, brushing, rotating, and generally TLC-ing it until it's ready to sell.

Affineur: A craftsman who stores and ages, or "finishes," a cheese. Small dairies or cheesemongers will send their formed, unripened cheeses to *affineurs* for refining.

Artisanal: A term describing cheeses and other food products that have been handmade in small batches using traditional techniques.

Cru: Made with raw, unpasteurized milk.

Curd: Milk that has coagulated or turned semisolid after the addition of rennet. The gelled curd is cut, depending on the style of cheese being made, into small, medium, or large curds.

Maître de fromage/fromager: A member of the restaurant staff who selects the cheese menu and can tell you more than you'll ever need to know about each cheese on the list, including wines to pair them with.

Paste: The edible interior part of a cheese, as opposed to the rind, or exterior.

Rennet: A substance found in the stomach of newborn milk animals that contains an enzyme called chymosin that reacts with lactic acid and causes milk to coagulate and curdle.

Tome, tomme, toma: Made with milk from more than one herd.

Whey: The watery liquid that separates from curds when they are cut and pressed.

The Cheese Course:
How to Fit *le Fromage* into a Full-Course Meal

Forget the fact that you've always eaten cheese and crackers as an appetizer. High-end restaurants offering a cheese course typically serve it in the European tradition, after the main course and before (or in lieu of) dessert. If the idea of a hunk of cheese showing up on a plate after your meal still conjures images of "wah-fer thin" mints and Monty Python, don't worry. The portions are wee by American standards and selected to complement your meal, not compound it.

*"Just like you don't open a meal with heavy braised
veal cheeks and end with a light crab salad,
a heavy cheese course isn't an appetizer. The palate
needs to build progressively into more intense and heavy
foods. In classic fine dining, cheese comes after the meat
course because it is strong and palate cleansing."*
—TODD GRAY, chef/owner, Equinox, Washington, D.C.

You don't have to memorize hundreds of varieties of cheese to choose the right mix for the course, either. In fact, because specialty cheeses require a lot of TLC, many restaurants offer only a composed selection of three to five cheeses.

MIX-N-MATCH CHEESE BOARD

When ordering a cheese board, most fromagers will recommend choosing cheeses that represent a variety of textures, flavors, and milks. That means selecting at least one cow, goat, and sheep milk cheese, aiming for a mix of soft or semisoft, firm, and hard cheeses, choosing some young, some aged, and with flavors that range from mild to sharp. If you want to get fancy, you might consider the origin of the cheese and select an international mix (French Saint André, Spanish Manchego, and English Stilton), or localize it to a specific region (Parmigiano-Reggiano, Taleggio, and Gorgonzola—all Italian cheeses). A restaurant with a fat list of cheeses will have the kind of staff who can tell you these details.

"You may see big cheese lists in restaurants in New York or San Francisco, but in the rest of the country, most restaurants offer composed courses of one, three, or five cheeses. It takes a lot of the guesswork and intimidation out of the equation. We want people to order it, not be afraid of it."
—KIM BADENHOP, chef/owner, Rendezvous Inn and Restaurant, Fort Bragg, California

CHEESE SERVICE

Depending on the restaurant's selection and your meal, a cheese course generally features one to five cheeses. Any more is overkill. The restaurant may offer a **cheese plate**, which consists of individual servings of each cheese, usually one to two ounces (about the size of your pinkie), arranged on a plate by flavor, from mildest to strongest. You should eat the cheeses in the set order instead of hopping around the plate because the stronger cheeses will overpower your palate and wipe out the mild, subtle cheeses.

On a communal **cheese board**, larger hunks of cheese are presented on a cutting board or marble slab for the table. Use your knife to carve bite-sized pieces from the cheese, starting with the mildest and moving to the strongest. You can use your fork, but most people use their fingers and serve themselves directly from the board. If a fork and a knife appear with your cheese course, use the utensils to slice and eat the cheese. Schmear the soft, creamy cheeses onto a bite of bread with a knife if you can't spear it with your fork, but eat the harder cheeses with a fork, *sans* bread. It's an uptight bit of etiquette, but in a fancy-pants restaurant, using those utensils keeps the smelly, oily cheesiness off of your fingers—and your wineglass, your shirt, and your date.

Cheese courses are usually served with extra tidbits, like slices of crusty bread, dried and fresh fruit, honey, nuts, olives, and fruit pastes. These bonus treats are a nice palate cleanser between bites, but purists say that eating cheese solo is the only way to get the full blast of flavor.

THE RIND: TO EAT OR NOT TO EAT?

Unless you've got a paraffin fetish, don't eat the wax. The rest is a matter of taste. Some people like the extra kick and texture the rind of an exquisite artisanal cheese offers. You've probably also seen people hack at a wedge of Brie until nothing is left but the white, velvety exoskeleton. But some cheeses are wrapped in chestnut leaves or rolled in ash, pine needles, or herbs for an aesthetic flair, so they might taste super-bitter. Enjoy with caution.

EAT THIS

The word *crottin* in the goat cheese Crottin de Chavignol means "horse poop" in French—a reference to the shape and size of the cheese, not the flavor.

Three Ways to Pair Wine and Cheese: The Making of a Great Match

Wine and cheese are perfect partners because they're both products of carefully controlled aging and fermentation. Even if you're on a budget, don't swap the wine for water if you're ordering a great cheese course. The combo of water and cheese causes indigestion.

Like any good marriage, the union of wine and cheese is happiest when there's a balance of characteristics that bring out the best qualities in both. You don't want a brute cheese like the blue-veined Spanish Cabrales competing with an acidic Sauvignon Blanc, or a creamy, earthy Toma losing its depth to a light, sweet German Riesling. So how do you choose wine for a course of five distinctly different cheeses?

#1: MATCH EACH CHEESE WITH A DIFFERENT WINE

This is the best way to get a true taste for wine-cheese pairings and, naturally, it's the most expensive. This is where the sommelier and fromager will come in handy. If your budget is tight, order tasting-size servings of wine, which are smaller and less expensive, and select three cheeses instead of five.

#2: MATCH REGIONAL WINES AND CHEESES

Unless agricultural geography is a hobby, this isn't the kind of information you'll have at your fingertips. Either ask the sommelier or fromager for good regional matches, or do your own homework. Instead of twiddling away hours on your computer playing Mah-Jongg, spend twenty minutes researching the origins of three of your favorite cheeses and see if you can link them to a particular wine that's made nearby. This works for many French, Italian, and Spanish wine-cheese matches. Some examples: Taleggio, a pungent, semi-soft Italian cow's milk, with Pinot Grigio, a light, crisp Italian white. Nutty Comté de Gruyère, made near Burgundy, with a Côtes du Rhône or Burgundy. Torta del Casar, a very soft, almost runny Spanish sheep's milk, with Ribera del Duero, a red Spanish wine.

"If you have wine left over from dinner, pick one cheese that goes great with that wine to finish off the bottle."
—MATT PARKER, The Cheese Stands Alone, Chicago

#3: MATCH THE STYLE OF THE CHEESE WITH THE WINE

Everything about the way a cheese feels and tastes comes down to how it is produced, which is also how it is classified. These categories provide a common denominator for making wine pairings.

Style: Unaged, rindless, fresh.

Cheeses: Chèvre, feta, Robiola, ricotta.

Wines that work: Dry Riesling, Pinot Blanc, Pinot Gris, Pouilly-Fumé, Sancerre, Beaujolais, Chenin Blanc, Vouvray.

Style: Soft-ripened, bloomy rind.

Cheeses: Triple-crèmes like Saint André, Brillat-Savarin, and Explorateur; Brie; Camembert; Toma.

Wines that work: Chablis, dry Riesling or Chenin Blanc, fruity Pinot Noir or Beaujolais. Bordeaux or Barolo won't overwhelm pungent varieties like Camembert.

Style: Washed-rind.

Cheeses: Epoisses, Livarot, Taleggio, Mahon, Munster, Pont-L'Eveque.

Wines that work: White Burgundy, Spätlese Riesling, Viognier, Grüner Veltliner, Pinot Gris, Beaujolais, Chianti, Barolo, Barbaresco.

Style: Natural rind.

Cheeses: Gruyère, Parmigiano-Reggiano, Manchego, Emmental, Romano, Raclette, Cheddar.

Wines that work: Pinot Noir, red Burgundy, Syrah, Beaujolais, Côtes du Rhône, Barolo, Barbaresco, Pinot Grigio, Chenin Blanc.

Style: Blue-veined.

Cheeses: Stilton, Cabrales, Maytag Blue, Roquefort, Gorgonzola.

Wines that work: Sauternes, tawny or vintage port, sherry, Madeira, Moscatel, late-harvest Riesling.

BE A BUFF

Cheese Primer, by Steven Jenkins; *The Cheese Plate*, by Max McCalman; *French Cheeses: The Visual Guide to More than 350 Cheeses from Every Region of France*, by Kazuko Masui and Tomoko Yamada; *The Cheese Course*, by Janet Fletcher

9

LOST IN TRANSLATION

the STATE of FINE DINING and MODERN CUISINE

Avez-vous faim pour plus? (That is, are you hungry for more?) Good food is a universal language everyone speaks, yet fine restaurants and fancy menus have a way of making many of us feel like mute foreigners. To become a local, or at least a savvy traveler, you need to polish up your culinary vocabulary, and that means learning a bit of French. As with noble grapes and divine wines, we owe a huge debt of gratitude to France for the mind-blowing food we eat in great restaurants. Many of the techniques and traditions that guide today's renowned chefs can be traced back to French culinary influences, from Catherine de Médicis' gastronomic overhaul of the French court to Escoffier's *Le Guide Culinaire* and Montagné's *Larousse Gastronomique*. Not too long ago, four-star ratings and true fine dining were pretty much exclusive to classic French restaurants. Period.

What's missing in this picture? The rest of the world, quite frankly. Where are the upscale Thai, Mexican, Vietnamese, Caribbean, Chinese, and Indian restaurants? They do exist, but they're more the exception than the rule. For every Arun's, the mecca of Thai fine dining in Chicago, there are thousands of downscale Thai eateries. The highly acclaimed Aquavit in New York serves fine Swedish food like, *literally*, no other restaurant in the United States. The Slanted Door in San Francisco serves up Vietnamese cuisine fit for royalty, but it's also one of a kind. The words *Mexican* and *fine dining* never appeared together in the same sentence in this country until chef Rick Bayless opened Topolobampo in Chicago. For the most part, restaurants specializing in ethnic cuisine tend to be of the casual, unstarched, and unstuffy variety.

However, the times are changing in fine dining. Just like stiff, tuxedoed maître d's, crystal finger bowls, and twenty-piece place settings have become relics of the past, so, too, has the idea that fine dining is strictly old-school European. Not only are fancy restaurants embracing global cuisines and the idea of casual fine dining— by focusing on top-notch service and food and toning down the starchy, intimidating formality—but exotic and ethnic restaurants are slowly gaining a foothold in the realm of fine dining. There are sensational upscale restaurants, like the ones mentioned earlier, that go far beyond the traditional French school of thought, but so far no other cuisine has established a reputation in culinary technique and tradition as completely as Japanese.

For the Mere Mortal, understanding the basics of classic French cuisine is fundamental to feeling confident and enjoying the fine dining experience—because France is where the Big Bang happened for fine food and service. Today, Japanese cuisine rivals French in terms of complexity, formality, and confusion to the modern fine diner, so familiarizing yourself with Japanese etiquette and cuisine, along with the nontraditional types of dining covered in this chapter, will help you round out your fancy restaurant education.

Classic French 101: Cookin' It Old School

Many menus, French and otherwise, assume you know what Flemish or Alsatian-style food is all about. How about a refresher, just to be on the safe side? Whenever you see the following words or phrasing on a menu, it's a safe bet that the dish will be prepared in a style based on ingredients and techniques associated with regional cuisines in France and Europe.

Cooking Styles *en France*

À l'alsacienne (al-zah-SYEHN), "in the style of Alsace," refers to braised meats with sauerkraut, potatoes, and sausage.

À l'anglaise (ahn-GLEHZ), "in the style of the English," means that the food is poached, boiled, or dipped in bread crumbs and fried.

À la bourguignonne (boor-gee-NYON), "in the style of Burgundy," typically involves meat braised in red wine.

À la flamande (flah-MAHND), "in the Flemish style," entrées are accompanied by braised cabbage, carrots, turnips, potatoes, and sometimes sausage.

À la Florentine (FLOHR-uhn-teen), "in the Florentine style," food sits on top of a bed of cooked spinach and is drizzled with a white sauce.

À la lyonnaise (ly-uh-NAYZ), "in the style of Lyon," refers to dishes featuring onions. Lyonnaise sauce is made with white wine, sautéed onions, and demi-glace.

À la niçoise (nee-SWAHZ), "in the style of Nice," applies to hot or cold foods served with black olives, garlic, anchovies, and tomatoes.

À la normande (nohr-MAHND), "in the style of Normandy," is fish and shellfish with mushrooms and truffles.

Normande sauce is velouté (a classic sauce) made with fish-based stock.

À la périgourdine (pay-ree-goor-DEEN), "in the style of Périgord," dishes are flavored or garnished with truffles. Sauce Périgueux is made with Madeira and truffles.

À la Provençal (proh-vahn-SAHL), "in the style of Provence," dishes usually include garlic, tomatoes, and olive oil, but may also use onions, olives, mushrooms, anchovies, and egg-plants.

FRENCH FOR "YUM"

You'll see the following cooking terms and preparations on many different menus, not just in a classic French restaurant, because chefs adapt some of the techniques for a range of cuisines. Plus, using words like *chemisé* on the menu makes the food sound très chic and much sexier than "wrapped in pastry."

À point (ah PWAH): to cook meat to medium doneness. It also refers to the stage when food is cooked to the perfect point of doneness and cooking is stopped, sometimes by dunking food in water, as with blanched asparagus or pasta al dente.

Au poivre (oh PWAHV): with black pepper, usually steak au poivre, or steak coated in black pepper.

Ballotine (bal-loh-TEEN): an entrée of meat, fish, or poultry that has been deboned, stuffed, rolled, tied in a bundle, and braised or roasted.

Broche (BROHSH) or **en brochette** (ahn broh-SHEHT): food that is spit-roasted on skewers.

Brûlé (broo-LAY): burned, like the burned sugar on top of crème brûlée.

Cassoulet (ka-soo-LAY): traditional slow-cooked dish of white beans, sausages, pork, and duck.

Chemisé (shuh-mee-ZAY): food wrapped or coated in pastry or sauce.

Chiffonade (shihf-uh-NAHD): literally "made of rags"; refers to thin-cut strips of vegetables used raw or sautéed to garnish dishes.

Civet (SIHV-iht or see-VAY): stew of game meat, usually rabbit, with onions, mushrooms, and red wine.

Cocotte (koh-KOT) or **en cocotte** (ahn koh-KOT): to cook in a round or oval casserole fitted with a tight lid.

Compote (kahm-POHT): fruit or vegetable that has been slowly cooked in a sugar syrup.

Concassé (kawn-ka-SAY): a coarsely chopped mixture.

Confit (kohn-FEE): meat that is salted and slowly cooked in its own fat, packed into a container, and covered in fat to preserve.

Confiture (kawn-fee-TYOOR): preserves or jam made by slow-cooking fruits or vegetables.

Consommé (KON-suh-may): fish or meat broth that has been clarified, or cleared of any sediment or haziness.

Coquille (koh-KEEL): served in a scallop shell or shell-shaped dish.

Coulis (koo-LEE): thick puree, sauce, or soup.

Court bouillon (koor bwee-YAWN): vegetable broth, typically used to poach fish.

Croquant (kroh-KAWN): crispy or crunchy.

Croûte (KROOT): French for "crust," refers to food wrapped in pastry and baked (en croûte), food served inside a round of hollowed-out bread, or toasted or fried bread.

Entrecôte (ahn-treh-KOHT): literally "between the ribs"; refers to a tender cut of steak, traditionally from between the ninth and eleventh ribs of beef.

Feuilletage (fuh-yuh-TAHZH): puff pastry; also *pâte feuilletée* (paht fuh-yuh-TAY).

Fumet (fyoo-MAY): concentrated stock, usually made from fish or mushrooms.

Galantine (GAL-uhn-teen): similar to a ballotine—a piece of meat, fish, or poultry that has been deboned, stuffed, rolled, and tied in a bundle, but is poached and served cold.

Glace de viande (glahs duh vee-AHND): meat juices boiled into a glaze.

Gratin (GRAH-tn): topped with cheese or buttered bread crumbs and baked until crispy brown.

Julienne (joo-lee-EHN): cut into matchstick-size strips.

Jus (ZHOO): meat, fruit, or vegetable juices; meat "au jus" is served in its own juices.

Maison (may-ZOHN): a specialty of the house, or house-made, like *pâté* or *saucisson maison* (soh-see-SAWN).

Marinière (mah-reen-YEHR): fish with wine and herbs; sauce made with fish-based stock.

Marmite (mahr-MEET): cookware used for slow-cooking stews, like cassoulet and pot-au-feu; it can also refer to food that is cooked and served in the same dish.

Marrow: the fatty meat found in the center of bones.

Meunière (muhn-YEHR): lightly dusted with seasoned flour and sautéed in butter.

Mirepoix (mihr-PWAH): carrots, onions, and celery diced and sautéed in butter; used to season sauces, soups, and stews.

Mousse: sweet or savory food or sauce (mousseline) that is made smooth and fluffy by adding whipped cream or beaten egg whites.

Paillard (PIE-yahrd): a grilled or sautéed thin slice of meat (usually veal, beef, or chicken).

Papillote or **en papillote** (ahn pah-pee-YOHT): cooked inside of a sealed envelope made of parchment paper.

Pâté (pah-TAY): seasoned ground meat, such as pork, liver, or veal, or fish or vegetables that have been finely chopped until smooth or coarsely chopped (as in country pâté) and cooked; usually served in a terrine (teh-REEN), a pork-fat-coated vessel.

Pâte à choux (paht ah SHOO): puff pastry made with eggs.

Pâte brisée (paht bree-ZAY): "short pastry" or crust made for sweet or savory quiches, pies, and tarts.

Potage (poh-TAHZH): pureed soup, usually thickened with cream or egg yolks.

Ragout (ra-GOO): thick meat, fish, poultry, or vegetable stew.

Rouille (roo-EE): a paste of hot chiles, garlic, bread crumbs, and olive oil, usually blended into fish stock or used to garnish fish dishes and stews like bouillabaisse (BOOL-yuh-BAYZ).

Roulade (roo-LAHD): thin pieces of meat rolled, stuffed, tied with string or secured with toothpicks, browned over high heat, then baked or braised.

Roux (ROO): a mixture of flour and clarified butter or oil, cooked for a few minutes (white roux), or until it is straw-colored (blond roux) or light brown (brown roux).

Saucisson (soh-see-SAWN): smoke-cured sausage.

Vol-au-vent (vawl-oh-VAHN): a small pot and lid formed from puff pastry, usually filled with meat in a cream sauce.

CLASSIC SAUCES

Fancy entrées can be swaddled in any one of countless complex and funky-sounding French sauces, but if you know just a few, including the four mother-of-all sauces—espagnole, velouté, béchamel, and allemande—you can flaunt your wisdom at the table.

Espagnole (ehs-pah-NYOHL) is a brown sauce made with beef stock, brown roux, mirepoix, herbs, tomatoes, and wine. Sauce bordelaise (bohr-dl-AYZ) is espagnole with the addition of red wine, shallots, and herbs. Demi-glace is reduced espagnole with sherry, port, or Madeira added.

Velouté (veh-loo-TAY) is white sauce made with white roux and veal stock. Sauce supreme is velouté finished with cream. Velouté can also be made with chicken (*volaille*) or fish (*poisson*) stock to make different sauces.

Béchamel (bay-shah-MEHL) is a white sauce of white roux, milk, mirepoix, and herbs. Mornay is a béchamel sauce with Swiss or Parmesan cheese added.

Allemande (ah-leh-MAHND), or Parisienne, is velouté sauce thickened with egg yolks.

Hollandaise, an emulsion sauce made with butter, egg yolks, and lemon, isn't technically a "mother sauce," but it is a base for several other sauces. Béarnaise is Hollandaise made with vinegar instead of lemon and flavored with tarragon or other fresh herbs.

Beurre blanc (burr BLAHN) is "white butter" sauce made with wine, vinegar, shallots, and butter.

Beurre noir (burr NWAR) is "black butter" sauce made by browning butter and adding vinegar or lemon, capers, and parsley.

"You will always see threads of the French influence in fine dining, but there's been a melding of global cuisines. The international influence, particularly the precision and pristine quality of ingredient that is the cornerstone of Japanese food, is having a huge impact on fine cuisine."
—PETER KASPERSKY, co-owner, Sea Saw, Scottsdale, Arizona

Japanese: The New School in Fine Dining

Once upon a time, foods from the Far East were little more than a freakish curiosity to Western diners—a sideshow of bizarre, spiky creatures served, eyeballs and all, in pungent, scary sauces and gelatinous slabs of raw fish to be eaten on a dare. Nowadays, the food our fathers called bait is glorified and consumed on a level that's on a par with fine French cuisine. While some of us are still loitering in the California rolls and shrimp tempura stage, curious but wary, many diners are barreling face-first into the unknown, gobbling sea urchin, eel, and other delicacies like blowfish. Whether you're a beginner or a brave-heart in the world of Japanese cuisine, you're still a *gaijin*, a foreigner with a few things to learn about the culture, the etiquette, and the cuisine.

TRADITIONAL JAPANESE CUISINE

For the record, "sushi" isn't a catchall word that encompasses any kind of Japanese food. There are many styles of Japanese cooking, from fried and grilled dishes to raw fish and one-pot soups. In Japan, restaurants specialize in one or two styles, but in the United States, you can find most of it under one roof.

Otsumami refers to beer snacks—any kind of salty, nibbly Japanese food you'd serve at a bar, like dried squid or cuttlefish (*surume*) and dried wasabi peas.

Teppanyaki is grilled meat or vegetable.

Sushi can be prepared several ways, but it always features rice seasoned with rice vinegar. *Maki* or *nori-maki* is a roll made of seafood, vegetables, and other fillings wrapped inside rice and a sheet of seaweed paper (*nori*) and sliced into rounds. Rolls can be thick (*futo-maki*), medium (*chu-maki*), or thin (*hoso-maki*). *Temaki* is a hand-roll—a cone of nori wrapped around rice, fish, and vegetables eaten, like an ice cream cone, from the hand. *Nigiri* is a slice of seafood dotted with wasabi and laid over a thumb-sized tuft of rice. *Chirashi* is sashimi, vegetables, and other bits like egg and mushroom served over rice. *Oshi* is seafood pressed into rice with a mold and cut into small pieces. *Inari* is rice and vegetables wrapped in fried tofu. Technically, *sashimi,* a plain slice of raw seafood, isn't sushi because it is not served with rice.

Tempura is seafood or vegetables coated in a light batter and fried.

Soba and **udon** are types of noodles, served cold or in hot broth with other ingredients like seafood, fish, vegetables, meat, and eggs. Soba are made from buckwheat and can be thick or thin; udon are made from wheat and are usually thick.

Yakitori are like kabobs—skewered and grilled meats and vegetables.

Katsu and **kushiage** are pieces of meat or seafood covered in panko (Japanese bread crumbs) and fried. *Katsu* or *tonkatsu* generally refers to pork, and *kushiage* is similarly fried seafood or vegetables served on skewers.

Kamameshi is a pot of rice steamed with your choice of a variety of meats, fish, or vegetables, like chicken, shrimp, oysters, mushrooms, and bamboo shoots.

Nabemono, one-pot meals, are a DIY, informal style of cooking an assortment of raw meats and vegetables in a communal pot of boiling broth over a burner set up at your table. *Shabu-shabu* and *sukiyaki* are examples of *nabemono*-style meals.

Robatayaki, or **robata** for short, is a Japanese style of grilling skewered meat, vegetables, fish, and seafood that have been lightly seasoned with salt, pepper, and *shichimi,* a hot pepper mix, over scorching-hot charcoals.

BE A SUSHI BARFLY

Japanese restaurants offer diners an opportunity that few others do: the chance to watch the chef work from a seat at the sushi bar. If you want to learn about the food, find out what's fresh, and occasionally earn a special treat, a front-row seat is the only way to go. Here's how to demonstrate that you're an eager, adventurous, and, most of all, respectful diner.

- **Don't try to impress the chef with what you know.** Be humble and curious. Watch him while he works and say, "That looks amazing. What is it?" or even "Can you make that dish for me? I've never had it."

- **Build rapport.** Being a regular helps, but if you're new to a restaurant, ask the chef if he has any off-the-menu specialties. Compliment his work. Offer him a beer or sake. But don't *expect* the royal treatment if you do these things. Do it out of respect and appreciation for the chef's craft.

- **Order sushi a few pieces at a time, sashimi first.** In a perfect world, you would eat each piece as it leaves the chef's hands. This isn't an option in most restaurants, so ordering two or three pieces per person at a time is far better than getting a giant sushi boat that takes twenty minutes to prepare and another twenty minutes to consume.

- **Use the Japanese word for the fish if you know it.** Menus usually list the English and Japanese words. Memorize your favorites from the following list.

Name That Fish

Speaking the language of sushi is a key part of gaining the respect of the chef—and probably some tasty freebies—and becoming an aficionado of the cuisine. (Avoiding those Americanized rolls stuffed with cream cheese, peanut butter, or mayo doesn't hurt either.) Take a minute to learn the names of a handful of the fish you order regularly. The good news is if you can read, you can pronounce just about anything in Japanese. When in doubt, pronounce everything phonetically, as in Maguro (mah-GOO-roe).

Maguro (tuna)

Toro (fatty tuna belly)

Shiro maguro (albacore)

Hamachi (yellowtail)

Katsuo (bonito)

Saba (mackerel)

Sake (salmon)

Tai (porgy, red snapper)

Hirame (halibut)

Suzuki (sea bass)

Unagi (freshwater eel)

Anago (sea eel)

Tako (octopus)

Ika (squid)

Awabi (abalone)

Mirugai (geoduck clam)

Torigai (Japanese cockle)

Aoyagi (Japanese red clam)

Akagai (pepitona clam)

Kobashira (small scallops)

Kaibashira (large scallops)

Kani (crab)

Ebi (cooked shrimp)

Ama ebi (raw shrimp)

Ikura (salmon roe)

Uni (sea urchin roe)

Tobiko (flying-fish roe)

Masago (capelin roe)

- **Ask—nicely—for fresh wasabi.** It's sweeter and less harsh than the sinus-singeing green wasabi paste most restaurants serve. It's worth the extra expense, and asking for it hints that you're not an amateur.

- **Slurping is A-OK.** It's impossible to lap up noodles in broth without a little noise. Plus, Japanese chefs consider it a compliment. It's also not rude to eat from a bowl of rice or soup held close to your mouth.

- **Think twice about sushi on Sunday or Monday.** Fish markets are typically closed on Sunday, so the fish you order is *at least* a day old.

"Do not mix wasabi in soy sauce! Japanese food, especially sushi, is very sterile and light. If you use too much wasabi or soy, you lose the flavor of the fish. It's okay to use real, fresh wasabi, which has a sweet aftertaste. It'll give you a little kick, but it's very important not to blow away the fish with something really spicy or salty."
—NOBUO FUKUDA, chef, Sea Saw, Scottsdale, Arizona

LAGNIAPPE

Spread the love in Japanese. To say a simple "thank you" to the chef, nod and say *dômo* (DOH-moh). Say *dômo arigatô gozaimasu* (DOH-moh ah-ree-GAH-TOH goh-zah-ee-MAH-soo) to express über-thanks. Insulted the chef or caused problems for the waiter? Say "sorry": *dômo sumimasen* (DOH-moh soo-mee-MAH-sehn).

STICKS AND STONES: JAPANESE ETIQUETTE

You won't get tossed out of a restaurant for committing any of these *gaijin* sins, but knowing basic etiquette shows respect for the chef, not to mention your worldly knowledge of Japanese table manners.

- Don't rub wooden chopsticks together. Pull any splinters off by hand.

- Don't stand your chopsticks in rice or pass food from chopsticks to chopsticks. These are funeral customs.

- Don't lay chopsticks on the table or bar. Lean the tips pointing left on the stone rest or across your soy sauce dish.

- Eat sashimi with chopsticks, but pick up sushi with your thumb and middle and index fingers.

- Don't put wasabi in your soy sauce. Dab it directly on the fish.

- Dip the fish side of sushi in the soy sauce, not the rice side.

- Eat sushi with sauce or frills, like scallions or ponzu, as is. Adding wasabi or dredging it in soy sauce is like pouring ketchup on French food. Trust the chef's preparation.

- Eat sushi in one bite. If it's too big, eat the second bite immediately—don't set down a half-eaten piece.

Wet Wipes

Most upscale Japanese joints offer customers a warm, damp towel, called *oshibori*, at the beginning of the meal. Do not wipe your face with it! Rub your hands clean before you dig in, then fold and lay it on the counter above the hand you'll eat sushi with. After you pick up pieces of *maki* or *nigiri*, use it to wipe your fingers.

COMPLIMENTS TO THE CHEF

Feeling adventurous? Order *omakase* (oh-mah-KAH-see), which means "entrusting" or, in a Japanese restaurant, "trusting the chef"—a multicourse meal of the chef's best fish and specialty dishes. In some restaurants, the courses keep coming until you call it quits. Other restaurants offer price points to choose from, which guides the type of fish the chef selects, but it won't affect the number of courses served. Unless you're a regular and the chef knows your preferences, give the restaurant at least a day or two of notice if you want to order *omakase*. This gives the chef time to prepare special tidbits and find rare fish the restaurant doesn't usually serve. Be sure to mention any dire food allergies when you make a reservation. Otherwise, give your dislike of mackerel or squid a rest for the night and let the chef work his magic without any limits.

LAGNIAPPE

Sound like a sushi pro: Politely ask the chef where the *uni* (OO-nee), or sea urchin roe, is from. If it's not from Santa Barbara, where the best stuff is hand-plucked from the ocean, take a pass.

Far East Feasts

Kaiseki-ryori (ki-SEH-kee ri-OR-ee) is a very traditional Japanese multicourse meal, similar to a chef's tasting. Although it was originally a light snack served during tea ceremonies, *kaiseki* has evolved into an elaborate series of five to fifteen small courses that Japanese chefs put together to show off the geography, natural elements, season, and local specialties of the region. Many Japanese chefs are trained to prepare traditional *kaiseki,* but don't put it on the menu because of the time and expense involved in preparing one. Plus, few diners here know what *kaiseki* is. If you're a regular or have a special occasion in mind, you might be able to talk a chef into preparing one for you. Give the restaurant at least a week's notice, and be prepared to pay a premium for the feast.

Everything You Need to Know About Sake (for Now)

You probably know that sake is made from rice, but is it wine, beer, or liquor? None of the above. Sake is not distilled, so it is not a spirit. It is made by fermenting rice, which puts it somewhere between wine and beer; wine, because it's fermented; beer, because it's made from a grain.

TALES OF THE FEAST

The first sake, called *kuchikami-zake* ("mouth-chewing sake"), dates back to around 300 B.C. Japan, and was made with the help of an entire village. People chewed rice, acorns, and millet and spit the mixture into a tub, where digestive enzymes from the saliva and the macerated grains would mold, break down into sugar, and ferment. Nowadays, sake brewers use *koji*, a mold enzyme that works like the saliva-grain mixture to convert the starch in rice to sugar.

To make sake, rice is polished or milled—a process called *seimai*—before it is fermented. The quality of sake depends mostly on how much the rice is milled. Polishing grinds away the outer layers of the grain, where there is a higher concentration of fats, proteins, and amino acids that can taint the flavor and aroma of sake. Closer to the center of the grain are the starches that ferment. Although there are exceptions, the more polished the rice, the more refined the sake, and the higher the quality. In the highest grades of sake, rice has been polished to remove at least 70 percent of the outer grain. As for wine grapes, there are different types of designated sake rice—about sixty-five varieties—and specific regions in Japan are known for growing the best quality of certain strains of rice. To order the best, look for one of the four premium sake styles. (Regular sake that falls outside this classification is called *futsushu* or *sanzoshu*.)

SPECIAL DESIGNATION SAKE			
Designation	Minimum Polish	Brewer's Alcohol Added	Qualities
Ginjo-shu *Daiginjo-shu*	60% 50%	Yes	Fruity, light to medium body, smooth, refined
Junmai ginjo *Junmai daiginjo*	60% 50%	No	Aromatic, complex, medium to full body
Junmaishu	70%	No	Acidic, strong, full-bodied flavor
Honjozo	70%	Yes	Light, smooth, fragrant

LAGNIAPPE

Shu means "sake" in Japanese. Although most Westerners pronounce it "SAH-kee," it is pronounced "SAH-keh" in Japanese. Any sake with the word *junmai* (JOON-my) in the name is made with rice only. No alcohol is added. *Dai* (DIE) means "great" in Japanese. As a prefix to the different styles of sake, it means that the rice has been polished to a minimum of 50 percent of the original grain size, and is considered the best.

HOT OR COLD?

Most premium sakes should be served chilled. Although some sake is fine at room temperature or warm—never hot—the heated stuff served in the United States is usually low quality. The reason for the debate? Before bottling and fermenting technology improved in the early 1900s, sake was brewed in wooden tanks, which gave the beverage a woody, rough flavor. Warming sake was a way to blunt some of the harshness. Today, brewers ferment sake in ceramic or glass, not wood. The delicate flavors and floral aromas in these premium sakes are at their best when served cool.

"Drinking from masu, *the small wooden boxes, is an old tradition dating back to the time when sake was brewed in wooden tanks and shipped in wooden casks. Today, the wood would mask the aromas and flavors of a premium sake, so it's better to avoid* masu *when drinking* ginjo *sake."*
—JOHN GAUNTNER, author of *The Sake Handbook*

Con-Fusion Cuisine: How to Approach a Fusion Meal

In world culture and politics, history has always demonstrated that conquering and ruling is the name of the game. Fortunately, in cuisine, sharing and blending is more the norm. The adventurous eaters among us embrace exotic cuisines, but our enthusiasm for daring and strange foods is nothing new. The cuisines of different cultures have bonded through the exchange of spices, fruits and vegetables, cooking principles, and equipment for centuries. In our lifetime, this practice has been given a fancy name: fusion.

Fusion cuisine is nothing more than a style of cooking that blends the techniques and ingredients of different cuisines. Naturally, classy restaurants have a more sophisticated and studied approach to the intermingling of foods, but in its purest sense, a turkey sandwich wrapped in a flour tortilla is fusion. So why all of the hubbub? Because great fusion food strives to be weird. Chefs concoct strange, intense, and contradictory combinations of flavors to astonish diners. They want you to think about the food you're eating and how it was prepared. They want to introduce you to food you've never heard of, much less tasted. Most of all, they want to shock and amaze you.

Even if some fusion cuisine is better in theory than in reality, the philosophy of innovation that drives great fusion is a bonus for any diner with a yen for exploring food. East meets West, North meets South, and every other imaginable collision of cuisines can happen, but therein lies the dilemma: Because there are no limits to the imagination and no geographical boundaries in this kind of food, there is no way to summarize the vast territory of fusion cuisine. If you're timid about trying new foods or unsure about some of the unruly combinations that show up on menus, take this advice for easing fusion confusion.

When Ordering Fusion . . .

- **Don't experiment on special occasions.** Birthdays and anniversaries aren't the time to find out you don't like French-Asian food, or that rice-paper ravioli gives you gas.

- **Do your research.** If you're clueless about Vietnamese cuisine, spend ten minutes online finding out the basics before you go to a Viet-Mex restaurant.

- **Scope out other tables.** Discreetly cruise the restaurant to see what other people are eating. Order by looks. This also gives you a general sense of the food so it's less of a shock when it shows up on your table.

- **Ask, ask, ask.** The waiter won't think less of you for not knowing what chayote or kombu is.

- **Tell, tell, tell.** If you don't get along with spicy-hot food or cilantro, be honest about what scares you and what you like so your waiter can steer you in the right direction.

- **Take baby steps.** Order small plates or appetizers instead of committing to one main course.

- **Save room for dessert.** As high-concept as some fusion restaurants are, you can usually count on one or two classic sweets on the menu.

- **Try, try again.** Don't give up on all fusion food just because one type isn't your bag.

Molecular Gastronomy: From Steak Foam to Inkjet Sushi, Today's Haute Cuisine

If conventional fine dining restaurants are the Louvres of the food world, a new genre of upscale restaurant is the artist's studio. Whereas the big, classic institution is all about preserving tradition and form and playing by a certain set of rules, this new spin in fine cuisine is about shattering conventions and showcasing the chef-artist's vision for what is now—and the future—in food. Today's haute cuisine, the newest twist in the cutting-edge world of good eats, is as much about science as it is about food. Part chemistry, part gastronomy, this global cuisine fuses technology, whimsy, cross-cultural ingredients, and cooking techniques in a way that would make Willy Wonka's head spin. This is a radical, new approach that makes the unthinkable—steak foam, exploding ravioli, freeze-dried foie gras, Parmesan air, and smoked bacon and egg ice cream—edible.

Although mad chef-scientist Ferran Adria, owner of the three-Michelin-starred restaurant El Bulli in Roses, Spain, is thought of as the founding father of this food movement, disciples and food radicals influenced by his work are tinkering in kitchen laboratories all over the world. To name a few: Wylie Dufresne of wd-50 in

New York City; Chicago's Grant Achatz of Alinea and Homaro Cantu of Moto; and Heston Blumenthal, the self-taught chef of the three-Michelin-starred Fat Duck restaurant in Bray, England. Like their haute couture counterparts, many far-out food trends will fade quickly, but some of the new techniques and culinary experiments pioneered by these chefs will leave a permanent mark on the way food is prepared.

EAT THIS

The term *molecular gastronomy* was coined by French scientist Hervé This and Nicholas Kurti, professor of physics at Oxford University, in the 1980s.

FOOD LAB

The new haute chefs put a surreal spin on cuisine by deconstructing unlikely ingredients using both traditional culinary techniques, like turning a tomato into jelly, or pioneering completely new methods, such as using flavored dyes in inkjet printers to make edible pictures. These are some of the terms you can expect to see on the menus.

Foams can be made with any liquid or food that can be liquefied (by pureeing and straining). The liquid is poured into a nitrous oxide–fueled whipped cream dispenser and chilled, then sprayed.

Infusions are like tea: An ingredient (herb, spice, fruit, vegetable) is steeped in a hot liquid, like water, broth, oil, or a sauce, to release the flavors.

Emulsions are made by quickly blending ingredients together in small drops so that they are completely merged and form a thick, silky sauce (think: oil + vinegar = vinaigrette).

Gelee or jelly takes its cue from Jell-O. A food is pureed or dehydrated and pulverized into powder, blended with gelatin and a liquid, like water or broth, and allowed to set.

Vapors are the semigaseous essential oils a food emits when it is heated to high temperatures without burning (which produces smoke). Chefs "capture" these vapors in airtight vessels and release the aromas on diners in elaborate food presentations.

"In classic fine dining, formality is part of the game. But when the waiter serves you a picture of pizza to eat, etiquette and formality are out the window. Sometimes we don't even give people the right utensils. We're serious about procuring high quality ingredients and preparing the food, but once it gets to the plate, we want diners to have fun with their food."
—HOMARO CANTU, chef, Moto, Chicago

Sous-vide, French for "under vacuum," is a process of cooking food in vacuum-sealed pouches in warm water. The method results in less shrinkage, a more natural texture, enhanced flavors, and a lower loss of nutrients than traditional cooking techniques.

ESOTERIC EATS

As unfathomable as the food is, you'll be relieved to know that in most of these restaurants, because everything from the preparation to the presentation of the food is so unconventional, you won't have to deal with a lot of uppity formality. No waiter will scoff at you for not knowing what braised pizza or hyacinth vapor is. The chef and waiters are more interested in taking you on a little adventure. As much as molecular gastronomy is about the food, it's also about entertainment. You're supposed to cut up and have a little bit of fun with it, so you need to go in with a different set of expectations. Here are a few pointers to get you in the right frame of mind for experimental dining.

- Control freaks, food-phobes, and picky eaters beware. The courses are the chef's picks, so don't take any bossy clients, and leave Grandma and the kids at home if they won't have fun letting someone else play with their food.

- Vegetarian? Shellfish allergies? Alternative courses are usually available to order on the spot, but let the reservationist know in advance. You may get better treats if the restaurant has more notice to shop for ingredients.

- *Fuhggedabout* substitutions. You cannot ditch ingredients or swap an item in a five-course menu with a better-looking dish on the ten-course menu. Don't even ask. Typical fancy restaurants may let you get away with nitpicking, but whimpering about the beets or tripe featured in a tasting menu will not go over well in these restaurants.

"You're not uncool or unsophisticated if you ask us questions. I do worry about diners not getting it, but if you only look at the individual ingredients or flavors on the menu, they're all pretty traditional. It just looks unconventional."

—WYLIE DUFRESNE, chef, wd-50, New York

BE A BUFF

The Fearless International Foodie: Conquers the Cuisine of France, Italy, Spain, and Latin America and *Conquers Pan-Asian Cuisine,* by David d'Aprix; *What's What in Japanese Restaurants: A Guide to Ordering, Eating and Enjoying,* by Robb Satterwhite; *The Sake Handbook,* by John Gauntner; *The Insider's Guide to Sake,* by Philip Harper; *A Taste of Japan: Food, Fact, and Fable/What the People Eat/Customs and Etiquette,* by Donald Richie

10

PALATE PREP

USING *all* FIVE SENSES *in a* CULINARY ORGY

You've got the credit card, the uncomfortable shoes, the natty, dry-clean-only duds, and an inkling of which wineglass and fork are yours—what more does a fine diner need? All five senses. No matter how much you learn about French cooking techniques or stuffy etiquette, once you're at the table your mind should be on the sensory experience and not quivering over place settings, wine lists, or what the Botoxed socialite at the next table thinks of you. Now is the time to let the anxiety go.

Usually, it's because we're in such a rush to fit in and not look like amateurs that we quickly order the overpriced and not-great bottle of wine or hurry through the menu without asking questions, and wind up feeling swindled or disappointed. The pace of fine dining is slower, and these restaurants expect you to take your time. That's why, more than anything, the real secret to mastering the art of fine dining and appreciating mind-blowing food is simply this: Slow down and engage all of your senses. You're less likely to fumble and will get more out of the experience if you let your senses adjust to and absorb every detail, from the look of the dining room, the staff, and the food appearing at other tables to the tinkling sound of glassware and the feel of a crisp linen napkin in your lap.

Your Best 'Buds: The Difference Between Taste and Flavor

When you're trying to hone your ability to pair wines or understand complex dishes, it's helpful to know the difference between **taste** and **flavor**. Taste receptors, or buds, are housed inside the tiny, bumpy papillae on your tongue. Technically, your tongue perceives only four "tastes": sweet, salty, bitter, and sour. *Umami* (oo-MAH-mee) is a fifth and slightly controversial taste sometimes referred to as "savory"; it is associated with meat, asparagus, cheese, tomatoes, and processed food.

For the last century people have generally accepted the idea of the tongue map, which set up boundaries on the tongue indicating where we register individual tastes. The belief was that we sense bitter on the back, sour on the middle, salty on the front, and sweet on the tip of the tongue. But the boundaries are a myth. Subsequent research has shown that we register all tastes all over the tongue, although some regions of the tongue may be more sensitive to certain tastes.

There are also different types of tasters among us. About 25 percent of us are supertasters, people who are very sensitive to bitter tastes and may also perceive sweet, salty, and sour more intensely. Supertasters tend to have a higher concentration of papillae on the tongue—particularly the tip—and may be the more finicky eaters in the group because of this increased sensitivity. Medium tasters, reportedly 50 percent of the population, are not as sensitive, and nontasters, about 25 percent of us, barely taste bitter or spicy foods at all.

FLAVOR SAVOR

With such a limited palate of four or five "tastes," how is it possible to distinguish between a lemon and a lime or a hot dog and filet mignon? Flavor, which we usually think of as the same as taste, is actually a collision of three sensations: taste, smell, and mouthfeel. **Taste**—bitter, sweet, salty, and sour—happens only on the tongue. **Mouthfeel** is the physical impression and texture food has in your mouth, such as the bubbles in Champagne, the tingling burn of hot chile peppers, the creamy richness of fresh butter, or the body of a big Cabernet Sauvignon. **Smell** is detected two ways: by sniffing food, called orthonasal olfaction, and by eating food, which pumps the odor from your mouth through the "back door" to your nasal cavity, called retronasal olfaction. (This is why, if you pinch your nose shut when you're chewing, the flavor of the food is muted. It's also why you should cancel your reservation if you've got a raging head cold.) Whether you're chewing a juicy piece of steak or trying an oyster for the first time, your brain processes all three sensations while a fourth dimension—the emotional element—kicks in. Whether you're conscious of the connection or not, flavor triggers personal, emotional information stored in your noggin that tells you "steak is good" because it reminds you of grilling out in the backyard or "oysters are weird" because the slimy, salty, ocean sensation brings back memories of a questionable fish taco you ate in Baja.

TALES OF THE FEAST

Women have a better sense of smell than men, and about two-thirds of supertasters are women. During pregnancy, these senses are heightened even more. The theory is that women developed these senses as a primitive survival technique to help them identify bitter plants and berries, which were usually poisonous.

Food Boosters: How to Enhance a Gourmet Feast

Genetics plays a huge role in your taste perception, and the emotional aspect of food and memory makes up the rest. Try as you might, you can't change your DNA or undo the food associations lodged in your memory, so you cannot willfully change your sensitivity to taste or flavor. However, according to Marcia Pelchat, Ph.D., a sensory scientist at the Monell Chemical Senses Center in Philadelphia, there are ways to enhance the sensory side of your meal and develop your palate.

- Anticipate and reiterate. Creating fond food memories is a key part of enjoying great meals. You do this by anticipating the meal and being able to recall details of the food you ate later. Tell the reservationist it's a special occasion. Dress up. Mention your plans to friends. Afterward, write an e-mail to a friend or pen a journal entry about the meal. The buildup to the meal, and remembering details in the aftermath, is as much a part of the experience as actually eating.

- Go hungry. Eat a light breakfast and lunch. A faint sense of hunger will build your anticipation of the meal, and you'll enjoy the food more if you're hungry.

- Test taste combinations. Every bite that goes into your mouth is affected by the taste of what was in your mouth before. The different tastes play off of each other in strange and surprising ways, and the more you experiment, the more adept you'll be at wine-food pairings and ordering courses that offer tasty contrasts and complements.

- Smell your food. One reason researchers believe cheeseburgers and pizza are such crowd-pleasers: You bring these whole, hot, aromatic foods to your mouth, right under your nose, to eat. The whammy of smell boosts the flavor.

Taste Makers

Ever notice that walnuts turn bitter with red wine? Or that bitter greens are less so if they're salted? Combining certain tastes (i.e., sweet, salty, bitter, and sour) can have a strange-but-true impact on the food you eat.

SWEET + SWEET = *LESS* SWEET

A bite of an über-sweet confection blocks any residual sugar in a dry wine, which will make the wine taste more acidic (sour). This is also why dessert wines taste less sweet (and pair well) with sugary desserts like crème brûlée or a fruit tart.

SALTY + BITTER = *LESS* BITTER

Sprinkle salt on grapefruit and the fruit will taste less bitter and more sweet. Salting leafy, bitter greens like frisee and radicchio will block some of the bite. Why? Salt tempers bitterness.

SOUR + SOUR = *LESS* SOUR

A sour taste, like vinaigrette, followed by another sour taste, such as an acidic Sauvignon Blanc, will flatten the taste of the wine.

SOUR + SALTY = *MORE* SALTY

Adding lemon (sour) to a barely seasoned fillet of fish will bring out more of the seasoning because sour enhances salt.

- Breathe when you chew. It's easy to forget to breathe when you're savoring a dreamy piece of Camembert or a tender sliver of Kobe beef, but breathing through your nose while you're chewing pumps more retronasal odors into your flavor factory. More odor means more flavor.

- Chew slowly. Let each bite roll around in your mouth so every sensory nook and cranny in your piehole experiences the flavor and texture of the food.

- Bounce around your plate. Your palate tends to get bored if bite after bite is the same, so alternate: a piece of pork, followed by a sliver of grilled onion, then a forkful of mashed potatoes. Skipping around gives your mouth and nose a variety of textures, tastes, and odors to absorb.

- Build diverse bites. Dynamic contrasts—when food changes sensations in the mouth, like ice cream going from solid and cold to melting and creamy—are more pleasing to the palate. Chefs orchestrate contrasts in the way they layer or prepare foods. Think of the crunchy or fried coating surrounding a soft filling or the grilled salmon stacked onto root vegetable puree with a crispy Parmesan wafer on top. Some of us also instinctively make our own contrasts, like when you spear a sautéed mushroom and a bite of steak on your fork. From the sauce to the sides, everything on your plate is part of a symphony of tastes, textures, and odors the chef chose to blend together. Don't be afraid to play with your food so that you get a little bit of everything in each bite.

Feed Your Mind: The Brain-Belly Connection

All of this information forms what we know as "taste" and "flavor," but it's the last bit—your emotional response—that makes eating more than just a series of chemical and physical reactions. Even in the realm of fine dining, eating is more about the communal ritual of sharing a meal and tapping into your own personal experience than it is about understanding the food. You don't need a gourmet's palate to appreciate an outstanding meal; you only need the right frame of mind.

BE A BUFF

A Natural History of the Senses, by Diane Ackerman; *Taste: A New Way to Cook*, by Sybil Kapoor; *How to Taste: A Guide to Enjoying Wine*, by Jancis Robinson

11

WHAT THE FOOD SNOBS KNOW

ubiquitous **CULINARY** *institutions in* **FINE DINING**

Food, like art, music, and politics, is a niche interest. There are people who approach eating and drinking with cultlike obsessiveness. They drive hours and cross oceans to try new restaurants. They are ravenous fans who follow dining trends and chefs like groupies, and gladly drop small fortunes on dinners. They are aficionados of regional cuisine, and hold dear their beliefs about where to find the best anything—pho, veal shanks, crème brûlée—in the world. These are people who plan their entire lives around the act of eating. Like all true diehards, they pride themselves in knowing the obscure history of good eats, the insider buzz of what's happening and who's who. Entry into this clique can take years of devotion to the subject of food, but you can hold your own in their company if you brush up on some of the names, history, and restaurants that define fine dining and the cult of the foodie.

Trendy Eats: Movements in Food History

Classic fine dining is its own institution. The starched tablecloths, mustachioed maître d's, and archetypal French-influenced menus are part of a long, established tradition many restaurants strive to achieve and preserve. But every now and then, there's a revolution. Some radical visionary steps in to give the old school something new to think about. These movements have a profound impact on the way things are done. Here's a look at what's been going on in the last thirty or so years of fine dining.

Haute cuisine (OHT kwih-ZEEN) is as fancy as it sounds. Like haute couture designers and their outlandish, expensive apparel, chefs use the finest ingredients to make the most elaborate, artistic, and ambitious food—and it ain't cheap. The chefs who succeed in this realm are innovators, perfectionists, and craftsmen who are revered in their field, like the late great chef of France's La Côte d'Or, Bernard Loiseau. His famous $267 Poularde Alexandre Dumaine, a chicken stuffed with truffles, is the perfect example of classic French haute cuisine: decadent, yet refined; elegant, yet over the top.

Nouvelle cuisine, "new cooking," refers to a lighter French style of cooking that surfaced in the 1970s. Eschewing the heavy, rich, creamy, and elaborately prepared dishes that define classic French cuisine, nouvelle chefs focus on authenticity of flavor and simplicity of preparation. Instead of relying on butter and flour, the movement inspired sauces made from meat juices, stocks, infusions, and reductions. Instead of drowning in heavy stews or braises, vegetables are quickly blanched or roasted to preserve their natural flavors. This is the movement that made it chic for chefs to put laughably minuscule portions of food on gigantic plates, but the ideas born from it—pristine ingredients served in a more natural way—are still around today.

Green cuisine is a by-product of the nouvelle principle, but takes the lighter, simpler approach to food even further: outside of the restaurant and into the environment. This movement espouses the virtues of artisanal edibles and organic, sustainable, and locally grown or raised foods as the path to gourmet enlightenment, health, well-being, and a safe, happy world. Although it's not an established term in fine dining the way that *haute* and *nouvelle* are—it still carries some tree-hugger, granola stigma—green cuisine represents a legitimate movement in the food scene.

Chef's Corner: Who's Who in Fine Dining

When you hear foodies talk about "Alice" or "Jean-Georges" with the kind of firsthand familiarity normally reserved for neighbors and family, they're talking about today's culinary icons. Some are famous for their contributions to the craft of cooking, and some are just infamous. The restaurant scene is in a constant state of flux, and both restaurants and chefs come and go, but a handful of contemporary chefs have made a lasting impact on the dining world. Here's what you need to know about who they are, what they're known for, and where they've worked.

CHEFS			
Chef	Locale	Restaurant(s)	Why You Care
Ferran Adria (feh-rahn ah-dree-AH)	Roses, Spain	El Bulli	The mad chef who gave us *Jetsons*-worthy foods like lobster foam and exploding ravioli spawned a new movement in high-concept food: molecular gastronomy.
Mario Batali (MAHR-ee-o bah-TAH-lee)	New York City	Babbo, Lupa, Po	For love of lardo and Northern Italy, Batali is the unlikely mascot for elegant Italian cuisine.

CHEFS

Chef	Locale	Restaurant(s)	Why You Care
Rick Bayless	Chicago	Topolobampo, Frontera Grill	Bayless elevated contemporary Mexican cuisine to the level of fine dining.
Paul Bocuse (boh-KOOZ)	Lyon, France	l'Auberge du Pont de Collognes	Awarded three Michelin stars and called "chef of the century," Bocuse is one of the fathers of nouvelle cuisine.
David Bouley (boo-LAY)	New York City	Bouley, Danube	A former Le Cirque chef, he brought Austrian cuisine into the mainstream with Danube.
Daniel Boulud (boo-LOO)	New York City	Daniel, db Bistro Moderne, Café Boulud	The award-winning French chef paid his dues at Le Cirque and was an early advocate of seasonal menus based on local ingredients.
Anthony Bourdain (boor-DAIN)	New York City	Les Halles	America's bad boy chef of great French bistro food and author of the warts-and-all memoir *Kitchen Confidential.*
Alain Ducasse (ah-LAHN doo-KAHS)	New York City	Alain Ducasse at the Essex House	The famed French chef pocketed a handful of Michelin stars for his restaurants in France before sharing his talent with America.

CHEFS

Chef	Locale	Restaurant(s)	Why You Care
Bobby Flay	New York City, Las Vegas	Mesa Grill, Bolo, Bar Americain	He put fine American Southwestern cuisine on the map and was one of the early celebrity chefs on the Food Network.
Thomas Keller	Yountville, California; New York City; Las Vegas	French Laundry, Per Se, Bouchon	His out-of-the-way restaurant became a destination in itself, and his tasting menu is legendary.
Emeril Lagasse (lah-GAH-see)	New York City, Las Vegas, New Orleans	Emeril's Delmonico, NOLA	His fondness for pork fat and the word *BAM!* made him a hit on the Food Network.
Nobu Matsuhisa (NO-boo MAHT-soo-hee-suh)	New York City, Las Vegas, Los Angeles, London	Matsuhisa, Nobu, Next Door Nobu	In his global restaurant outposts (Robert De Niro is a partner), he fuses classic Japanese with South American cuisine.
Danny Meyer	New York City	Union Square Café, Gramercy Tavern	An early supporter of farmer's market–based daily specials, he kick-started casual fine dining: service and upscale food without the attitude.
Rick Moonen	New York City	restaurant rm	Safe, sustainable seafood is his culinary mission.
Masaharu Morimoto (mah-sah-HAH-roo moh-ree-MOE-toe)	Philadelphia	Morimoto	A Nobu graduate and the third (and final) Japanese Iron Chef in the spin-off of the popular Japanese series.

CHEFS

Chef	Locale	Restaurant(s)	Why You Care
Charlie Palmer	New York City	Aureole	A pioneer of progressive American cuisine, he makes classic French fare using American artisanal foods.
Jacques Pépin (zhahk pep-ANN)	New York City		Acclaimed French chef and Julia Child's co-star, he is currently the dean of special programs at the French Culinary Institute in New York City.
Wolfgang Puck	Los Angeles; Las Vegas; San Francisco; Maui, Hawaii	Spago, Vert, Chinois	The Austrian chef who introduced the world to gourmet pizza in his swanky Hollywood eatery is now a global brand.
Eric Ripert (REE-pair)	New York City	Le Bernardin	Known for his breathtaking food presentations, he helms the kitchen of the highly acclaimed French seafood mecca.
Marcus Samuelsson	New York City	Aquavit, Ringo	He is a pioneer chef of fine Scandinavian cuisine.
Masayoshi Takayama	New York City, Los Angeles	Masa, Ginza Sushiko	His restaurant Masa is the first to receive four stars from the *New York Times*—a huge leap for Japanese fine dining.

CHEFS

Chef	Locale	Restaurant(s)	Why You Care
Jacques Torres	New York City	Le Cirque 2000	Award-winning French pastry chef, a.k.a. Mr. Chocolate, turns dessert into art and vice versa.
Charlie Trotter	Chicago	Charlie Trotter's	The acclaimed chef's seventeen-year-old restaurant never ages; the menu evolves as an homage to organic, seasonal, and heirloom foods.
Jean-Georges Vongerichten (ZHAN-zhorj vohn-gerh-ICK-ten)	New York City, Hong Kong, Las Vegas, Shanghai	Jean Georges, JoJo, Vong, Spice Market, (The Mercer) Kitchen	The trendsetting chef inspires awe and accolades for his reinterpretations of classic French cuisine.
Alice Waters	Berkeley, California	Chez Panisse	She's the Mother Chef of the organic, local, and sustainable food movement.

THE FOREFATHERS OF FINE DINING

What Ben Franklin and Thomas Jefferson are to the Constitution, these guys are to fine dining.

Antoine Beauvilliers (boh-vee-YAY) was the French chef who opened the first real restaurant in Paris, called La Grande Taverne de Londres, in 1782. In 1814, he published *L'Art de Cuisinier*, one of the premier books on the technical science of cooking, management, and service. He cowrote *La Cuisine Ordinaire* with Antoine Carême. A French almond cake is named after him.

Jean Anthelme Brillat-Savarin (bree-YAHT SAV-uh-rihn) was a French lawyer-turned-gourmand who wrote about the culture and science of cooking in *The Physiology of Taste: Or, Meditations on Transcendental Gastronomy*, published in 1825. Blending history, personal stories, and pithy observations on the higher calling of food with the brass-tacks mechanics (and chemistry, anatomy, medicine, and physics) of cooking, the book was a monumental dissertation on food. It is chock-full of his famous, quotable quips, like "Show me what a man eats and I will show you who he is."

EAT THIS

Brillat-Savarin is a creamy cow's milk cheese named for the famous gastronome, no doubt for his declaration that "a meal without cheese is like a beautiful woman with only one eye."

Marie-Antoine Carême, the pioneer of grande cuisine, was the first bona fide celebrity chef. In the early 1800s, the French cook and *patisseur* used his knowledge and passion for architecture to make structurally elaborate, purely decorative food displays—bridges made of sugar, pedestals of towering pastry, whimsical constructions of edible art—at banquets for the rich and fabulous. He is part of the reason you're served gravity-defying stacks of food, fancy garnishes, and dramatic swirls of sauce that are *almost* too pretty to eat in froufrou restaurants today.

George Auguste Escoffier (es-KOF-yay) was an influential French chef world-famous for his command of the Savoy and Carlton luxury hotel restaurants in London, but he holds a place in the heart of all chefs for his book *Le Guide Culinaire,* a meticulous collection of modern French recipes and cooking principles first published in 1903. If you want to know what's in sauce aurore or how chefs make authentic *tripes à la mode de Caen,* this is the place to find it. (English edition: *Escoffier: The Complete Guide to the Art of Modern Cookery,* translated by H. L. Cracknell and R. J. Kaufmann.)

Prosper Montagné was a legendary French chef most known for his monolithic encyclopedia of French gastronomy, *Larousse Gastronomique,* published in 1938. The book has been updated periodically and translated into English, and it is an invaluable resource for anyone with a keen interest in the culture and history of food.

BORN IN THE U.S.A.

Frenchies get all of the credit for the birth of fine cuisine, but we've got a few homegrown food heroes, too.

James Beard was the father of American gastronomy. His writings, teachings, and culinary work established the importance of American cuisine (previously thought of as the bland, canned, ready-made drek of the post–World War II era) in the 1950s. Today, the James Beard Foundation (www.jamesbeard.org) carries on the preservation of American food heritage by offering scholarships to people pursuing a career in the culinary arts and doles out annual awards to restaurants, chefs, writers, and other professionals in the foodie industry.

M. F. K. Fisher, a passionate and charismatic food writer, was highly influenced by Brillat-Savarin's work (she translated his book, *The Physiology of Taste,* into English in 1949) and penned similarly witty and sharp culinary essays and autobiographical and historical meanderings about food, including *The Art of Eating* and *How to Cook a Wolf.* One of many food-isms attributed to her: "Sharing food with another human being is an intimate act which should not be indulged in lightly."

Julia Child introduced the average American to French culinary techniques in 1961 with her cookbook *Mastering the Art of French Cooking,* but it was her 1963 television series *The French Chef,* along with her unmistakable warble and quirky, unfussy style, that cemented her celebrity. She published several classic cookbooks, including *The Way to Cook,* and hosted a handful of television cooking shows over the years. She is often credited with taking the snobbery out of fine French food and single-handedly broadening the American palate.

Culinary Schools and Organizations: Fundamental Food Institutions

French Culinary Institute: With a focus on classic French technique and a mindfulness toward American cuisine, this culinary and pastry arts school turns out some of the top chefs in the United States with the help of faculty like Jacques Pepin and Jacques Torres. L'Ecole, the school's restaurant, is open to the public and the prix fixe and à la carte seasonal menus are prepared by students (under supervision)—an ideal setting to hone your own fine dining skills. www.frenchculinary.com

Culinary Institute of America (CIA): The oldest culinary school in America, founded in 1946, is located on the Hudson River in Hyde Park, New York. A second campus, the Culinary Institute of America at Greystone, is in St. Helena, California. Graduates include *Gourmet* magazine editor Sara Moulton, Anthony Bourdain, Rick Moonen, and Rocco DiSpirito. www.ciachef.edu

Le Cordon Bleu: Founded in Paris in 1895, it is one of the oldest and most prestigious culinary institutions in the world, with twenty-six international schools in fifteen countries and thirteen certified programs taught at cooking and hospitality schools in the United States. Julia Child graduated from Le Cordon Bleu in Paris. www.cordonbleu.net

Slow Food: Founded in Italy in 1986 by Carlo Petrini, Slow Food is an international movement spreading the good word about indigenous culinary traditions, like artisanal cheeses and other handcrafted foods, heritage animal breeds, and heirloom fruits and vegetables, which are threatened by industrial agriculture and mass food production. www.slowfood.com

Sustainable Table: This consumer education campaign aims to increase awareness of organic, sustainable food production. The organization publishes the Eat Well guide, a national online directory of restaurants, farms, and markets that sell sustainably raised meat, poultry, eggs, dairy, and produce. www.sustainabletable.org

Chef's Collaborative: This collective of chefs works to educate the public and other food professionals about eating locally grown, artisanal, and seasonal foods. The group produces two guides to help consumers and chefs make better choices in restaurants: the Sustainable Seafood Primer and the Chef's Collaborative Restaurant Guide. www.chefscollaborative.org

Find Dining: Guides to Fancy Restaurants

If you're looking for a hit-list of top restaurants, these established guides are the source.

Michelin Red Guide—first published in 1900 by French tire magnate Andre Michelin as a marketing tool to encourage people to burn rubber—is a traveler's hotel and restaurant guide for road-trippers in Europe. The Red Guides send a small legion of anonymous (and famously stealthy) inspectors to assess thousands of restaurants across Europe. Each review is a spartan two- or three-line summary dotted with the guide's signature reference symbols, like the crossed fork and knife and the Michelin Man, but restaurants and diners know the guide for its coveted one-, two-, and three-star ratings. True to its roots, the Guide's star status is tied to the idea of car travel: One star rates as "a good place to stop" during your travels, two stars warrants "a detour," and three stars merits "a special journey." Don't let the understated ratings fool you. Earning or losing a star has been known to make or break serious restaurants, and less than 10 percent of the 18,000-plus restaurants reviewed receive any star at all. The first Red Guide to New York City, the only non-European destination on the roster of cities, was published in 2005. Trivial fact: The jovial, roly-poly Michelin Man is named Bibendum. www.viamichelin.com

Guide Gault-Millau (goh mee-YOH) and **Gayot** (guy-OH) publish slightly more detailed and sassy reviews than Michelin and rank restaurants in the United States and internationally with white tocques (chef's hats), but judge on the quality of the food alone, not service, décor, or ambience. Trivial fact: The Gault-Millau and Gayot guides were launched by Henri Gault, Christian Millau, and Andre Gayot, food critics who coined the term *nouvelle cuisine* in the seventies. www.gayot.com

Zagat Survey (zah-GAHT) guides are packed with refreshingly and sometimes brutally honest appraisals and useful tips from *actual diners*—not paid reviewers. This family of guides rates restaurants in metropolitan areas in the United States and abroad on food, décor, service, and cost. If you can get past their awkward use of random direct quotes pulled from surveys, the summaries can help steer you away from impossibly snooty, overpriced, and overrated restaurants, and the guides cross-reference listings by neighborhood, cuisine, and "special features" (think: fireplaces, tasting menus, and celebrity chef restaurants). Trivial fact: The first Zagat Survey, published in 1979, covered New York City restaurants. Today, the survey covers more than seventy cities, and 250,000 people vote. www.zagat.com

2005 Top Restaurants from Zagat Survey

BOSTON

Oishii	Lumière
L'Espalier	Hamersley's Bistro
Aujourd'hui	Salts
Il Capriccio	Coriander
Olio	Caffe Bella

CHICAGO

Ritz Carlton Dining Room	Ambria
Tallgrass	Mirai Sushi
Les Nomades	Seasons
Carlos'	Charlie Trotter's
TRU	Le Titi de Paris

LOS ANGELES

Sushi Nozawa	Angelini Osteria
Matsuhisa	Joe's
Water Grill	Sushi Sasabune
Mélisse	Spago
Saddle Peak Lodge	Katsu-ya

MIAMI

Chef Allen's	Joe's Stone Crab
Shibui	Cacao
Nobu Miami Beach	Osteria del Teatro
Norman's	Ortanique on the Mile
Tropical Chinese	Romeo's Cafe

NEW YORK CITY

Le Bernardin

Bouley

Daniel

Gramercy Tavern

Sushi Yasuda

Next Door Nobu

Nobu

Jean Georges

Peter Luger

Alain Ducasse

SAN FRANCISCO

Gary Danko

French Laundry

Masa's

Fleur de Lys

Le Papillon

Sushi Ran

Caf La Haye

La Toque

Acquerello

Chez Panisse

WASHINGTON, D.C.

Makoto

Inn at Little Washington

Maestro

Citronelle

L'Auberge Chez François

Marcel's

Gerard's Place

Restaurant 2941

L'Auberge Provençal

Obelisk

BE A BUFF

Slow Food: The Case for Taste, by Carlo Petrini; *Larousse Gastronomique,* by Prosper Montagné; *The Physiology of Taste,* by Jean Anthelme Brillat-Savarin; *Le Guide Culinaire,* by George Auguste Escoffier; *The Art of Eating,* by M. F. K. Fisher.

12

EATIQUETTE

DEAR MORTAL: *things your* **MAMA** *probably* **TAUGHT** *you*

(BUT YOU FORGOT)

Q. *I've seen everything from jeans and sneakers to sequins and bow ties in restaurants. If I go to a snazzy dinner on a date or with a bunch of friends, as long as I'm clean and I can pay the bill, does it really matter what I wear? Can I wear casual clothes?*

A. You can pay the bill, but you can't afford a shirt with buttons? Or pants that you wouldn't wear to the gym? If you have to ask the question, your idea of "casual" probably isn't appropriate. When you're dining in a high-end restaurant, think of yourself as a guest in a VIP's well-staffed home. Put yourself in *their* Manolos. If you were throwing a dinner party and sparing no expense, would you want your guests in your version of "casual" clothes or a little more dressed up?

When in doubt, call ahead to find out if a jacket and tie are required for men, which should also indicate how fancy their dress code is. Flush or broke, you don't have to sweat your fashion sense or lack of designer labels. Just wear dress shoes, a skirt, pants, collared shirts—anything you'd wear to a nice wedding, or a funeral. Bottom line: If you want to *get* in, you should *fit* in.

Q. *I so want to bring my sweet baby/toddler/preschooler to a four-star restaurant. It's sort of an* Eloise *fantasy of mine—having the world see how terribly sophisticated and charming my child is. How do fancy restaurants feel about bringing along the brood?*

A. Few restaurants will tell you *not* to bring your precious offspring, but it's a good sign they're not welcome if they don't have a kid's menu. Truthfully, it's for you to decide whether your wee ones can handle the outing without turning into savages by the second course. If they're prone to teary meltdowns or if they're finicky eaters who won't be able to order off the menu—because it's *not* okay to ask a four-star chef to make chicken nuggets for your tot— leave your bundle of joy at home. You'll spend less on a babysitter and pizza, and spare your fellow diners the potential ugliness—not to mention guarantee your own peace of mind.

Even if yours is an absolute angel, tell the restaurant you're bringing a pint-sized guest so that they can accommodate you. You get points for exposing your young'uns to the finer things in life; just make sure junior is ready for it.

Q. *Is there any way to ask to change tables without feeling like a twit? I can't stand sitting next to big parties because they're usually loud, but I hate to make a scene by moving to another table.*

A. Spare yourself from the table shuffle walk of shame by revealing your persnickety seating issues when you make the reservation so the host or maître d' can work out the table arrangements before-hand. If it's too late and you find yourself in a bad table way, you don't have to suffer in silence. However, like any awkward request that has the potential to make you look like an ass, it's all in the de-livery. If you address the waiter like it's *his* fault that the obnoxious guy at the next table can't hold his liquor or the direction of your chair isn't properly feng shui-ed, you *should* feel squirrelly. If you want to switch the seating arrangement, for whatever reason— noise, smoke, a draft, the sun in your eyes—you have to act like you realize just how ridiculous it is. Say, "I know this may be a hassle, but is it possible to change tables?" and quietly explain the problem to your waiter. Give the waiter a chance to fix the situation and, depending on how packed the restaurant is or how important moving is to you (think: tip), the restaurant should try to accommodate your request. If the place is slammed and no tables are available, bring the issue to your waiter's attention anyway and hope for the best. They might comp your appetizers or give you a free dessert for handling the situation graciously.

Q. *When on those rare occasions I do have enough money to spend on a nice meal, I don't want to pay $20 for a fancy bottle of water thawed from a snowbank in the Swiss Alps. When the waiter asks "flat or sparkling?" will I sound like a cheapskate if I say "tap"?*

A. Tap water, toilet water—if you ask for it, your waiter should pour it up without a hint of haughtiness. It's your dime, and if your waiter pushes the up-sell ("May I interest you in some Pellegrino? It's an *excellent* palate cleanser") or says, "We only serve bottled water," you're entitled to shave the tip for pretentious service.

Q. *I like to try as many things on a menu as possible, but I don't have a food critic's budget. Restaurant portions are oversized, anyway, so I usually ask to have entrées split, and I'm always picking off of other people's plates. Is sharing considered rude, and do restaurants hate people who split meals?*

A. Whether it's budget or bulge that's driving your decision, ordering one entrée to share with the whole table is not a great way to win points with your server or a restaurant, particularly on busy Friday and Saturday nights. You're taking up prime real estate for two or more diners, but ordering for one, so the restaurant *and* waiter lose money. However, few restaurants will refuse to let you split a dish. Some may charge you a small fee, as well. If you simply want a taste of your date's braised lamb chop or want to order two full entrées and go halfsies so you can experience more of the menu, "sharing" is not a problem. In either case, tell your waiter, "We'd like to split this dish." You'll know you're in a spot-on restaurant if the order comes out halved and served on two plates.

It is not strictly proper to eat directly from another diner's plate. If the dish isn't split for you, the waiter should set an extra plate. Use it. Cut and set any shared bits on the plate and serve yourself from it. If your bill comes with no additional service fee, you should give a larger tip (say 20 to 25 percent) for sparing you the problem of hacking an expertly prepared meal in two and for the great service despite the lower tab.

Q. *Unless I drench my food in something vinegary or spicy, it all pretty much tastes the same. Fortunately, I like the taste of condiments, but people act like I'm committing a mortal food sin by asking the waiter for ketchup or Worcestershire sauce. What's the problem?*

A. Foodies and the people who get hyper about proper etiquette say that when you're at a dinner party in someone's home, asking for condiments and seasonings that aren't set on the table is taboo. But when you're paying for a meal, the rule isn't so black and white. The fact is, once your plate hits the table, it's yours to tinker with. A chef might cringe at the thought of diners dousing his master-pieces with hot sauce, but if you need something extra to make your meal more enjoyable, ask away. However, to be polite, taste the food before you make such a request. You may find that you don't need to tweak the chef's creation.

Q. *In some restaurants, it takes the waiter several trips to deliver all of the plates to the table. It seems absurd to wait until everyone is served, particularly because I don't want my food to get cold and it's just a matter of seconds before their food shows up. Is it rude to start eating?*

A. Upscale restaurants should make this a nondilemma by serving the entire table at once. If your dish arrives seconds or minutes before those of other diners at your table, it is common courtesy to wait until everyone is served. If the host of the meal, the guest of honor, or your date/dinner pal recognizes that you're waiting and says, "Hey, don't wait for me. Please, dig in," it's okay to start eating. If you are the host or guest of honor and others at the table are waiting, keep your mitts off of your fork and knife until at least one other dinner companion is served. Even if your guests say, "Don't wait for us," you shouldn't start without them. All rules are moot if you order an appetizer or a dinner salad and your fellow diners do not have a first course coming. You may start eating as soon as everyone who ordered a course is served.

Q. *Is it ever okay to eat with your hands in a fancy restaurant? If I order half a roasted chicken and meat is still stuck to the bones after I've fork-and-knifed it, I really, really want to pick up a leg or wing for a nibble. I don't want to look like a caveman, but it doesn't seem fair to leave some of the best pickin's on the plate.*

A. Swanky restaurants tend not to serve those finger-lickin' foods requiring bibs or wet wipes, like ribs, wings, and fried chicken. If the restaurant offers a posh version of these picnic standards, or a whole roasted chicken, squab, or other small poultry, you should eat as much as possible using your fork to hold the bone while you cut meat away with your knife. It is not rude to nibble the remaining bits if you hold the bone between your thumb and index finger. Just don't grasp the food in your fist, gnaw on the bone, or insert the bone into your mouth and use your teeth to shuck away the odd bits of meat.

Bones from steaks and chops, like a porterhouse or a pork chop, should never be picked up and inserted in your mouth even if there are tasty and hard-to-reach morsels left over. Use your fork and knife to sever meat from the bone. One exception: Bones that have been frenched, where meat is cut away to reveal the bone (as with a rack of lamb), are prepared that way because (1) it looks neat and (2) it gives you a nice, clean handle to pinch between your fingers. Other foods that are finger-approved: artichoke leaves, crispy bacon, unsauced asparagus stalks, olives, cornichons (small pickles), corn on the cob, strawberries with stems attached, and the shell from whole lobster and crab (but pick and eat the meat with a fork, not your fingers). If you can easily manage any of these items with a fork and knife, do. Also, it is not polite to nibble food speared on your fork, such as asparagus or *frites*. Don't lift anything on a fork to your mouth if you can't eat it in one bite.

Q. *I order meat and fish cooked medium-well or well-done, but many times I cut into a steak and see too much pink. I hate sending food back because I imagine the cooks having their way with my meal if I complain. Would it be wrong to order something entirely different if my first order gets screwed up?*

A. Approach any potentially awkward or contentious complaint in a restaurant with one thought in mind: You catch more bees with honey than with vinegar. Don't yell at the waiter or cop an attitude. Don't behave as though the kitchen screwed up your order on purpose. Don't consume half of your steak (or any food or wine you intend to return) and then send it back. It's okay to be disappointed, but bad attitude makes a bad situation worse. You want the waiter to feel sorry for you and, if possible, sorry enough to comp a free drink or dessert. That's not going to happen if you're tense and confrontational.

Get straight to the point—politely—by saying, "I hate to be a bother, but I think my tuna steak is undercooked. I ordered it medium-well." Period. Don't go into grand detail about why you hate rare fish or meat or how this kind of thing always happens to you. The waiter should apologize and take your plate away with the promise of correcting the problem and/or removing it from your bill. In general, if it's an easy fix (e.g., cooking your fish longer) and there's nothing so seriously wrong with the food that it can't be returned—as in, spoiled, overcooked, or covered in an ingredient you're allergic to—don't try to order a different entrée. At this level of dining, you shouldn't worry about your food getting mopped across the floor or licked by a surly sous-chef if you have a legitimate complaint. If you have another complaint, such as the food being too salty or spicy, and the waiter insists the item is prepared the way it always is, kill 'em with kindness. The more diplomatic and calm you are when you navigate these gray areas of complaints, the more likely the waiter will go out of his way to make you happy.

However, if you send back food or wine because your complaint is "I thought it would taste different" or "I didn't realize habanero peppers were so spicy"—in other words, if it's *your* problem and not the restaurant's—you can still send it back and order something else. Just don't expect the restaurant to knock the dish off your tab.

Reasonable Returns

A restaurant should fix these legitimate food and wine issues, usually by replacing the item or removing it from your bill.

- Corked or oxidized wine

- Under- or overcooked meat (provided you ordered it "well" or "rare")

- GUFO (Gross or Unidentifiable Foreign Object) in your food

- Mistakes in the order, such as sauce on your dish if you asked for "no sauce"

- Cold food that should be hot and vice versa

- Items you're allergic or averse to that weren't listed in the menu description

Q. *I always assume the waiter will clear any flatware or plate between courses and set new pieces for each course, but I've been in fancy restaurants where the waiter takes the knife and fork from my plate and lays them on the table. How do I know when to keep or give up used tableware?*

A. In classic fine dining, it is standard practice for waiters to clear any used tableware, including plates and flatware, and to replace it with the appropriate tools for the next course. Today, there's a newish phenomenon known as casual fine dining, where the service and food are still top-notch, but the atmosphere is a little more laid-back. There's less of the rigid formality normally associated with true fine dining, like the coat-and-tie policy for men and the practice of clearing all tableware. It can be confusing, but the flatware dilemma is an easy one to solve. Just lay your fork tines up and knife blade in (business edge angled facing you) on your plate with the handles resting at five o'clock when you are finished eating, and let your waiter take the lead.

Q. *I've read about restaurants with tasting menus that are so long, the meal lasts four or five hours. I can't sit in one place for more than an hour without getting fidgety. Plus, I'm a smoker. Is it rude to leave the table between courses?*

A. Restaurants put midmeal smokes and bathroom breaks in the same category: They're both bodily functions that need to be attended to in order for you to have a great meal. The number one rule in all questions of etiquette is making sure others are comfy and happy. If you're squirming in your seat because you need to make a pit stop, stretch your legs, or take a few puffs, your discomfort isn't just your problem. The people at your table watching you shift and fidget aren't comfortable, either. As long as you're not jumping out of your chair for a smoke break every five minutes, you can leave the table for any reason. Just don't expect the waiter to hold your order while you smoke or dawdle. Tell the server if you're headed to the bar to smoke, and ask to be retrieved if your food arrives.

Q. *I get that yacking on your cell phone and belching are things you don't do at the table, but what about something more discreet, like applying lipstick or blowing my nose? I can do these things in the blink of an eye, and the whole process of excusing myself to go to the bathroom causes more of a disturbance.*

A. There are some things you just don't do at the table, whether or not someone will witness your behavior and no matter how quickly or discreetly you can pull it off. Short of dabbing your lips and fingers with your napkin, all forms of primping, rearranging, blotting, wiping, scratching, adjusting, or blowing should take place away from the table and other diners. Always. No exceptions. If you have a sneezing fit, contract a raging case of the hiccups, or need to "fix" yourself in any way, it takes two seconds to excuse yourself from the table. Think of it as another opportunity to check your breath and make sure you don't have spinach or black pepper rammed between your teeth.

Q. *Restaurant portions can be huge, and I hate to let such fine—and expensive—food go to waste. Is it okay to ask for a doggie bag, or are there some situations when you should let a good thing go?*

A. Asking to have your leftovers "wrapped up" or "to go" might sound more classy than asking for a "doggie bag," but that's your call. Most chefs probably would prefer to see their masterpieces go home with you in a Styrofoam box than into the garbage. But you should also think about whether the one or two leftover scallops or that single baby lamb chop will survive the move to your refrigerator. A big hunk of steak and mashed potatoes might reheat, but many other dishes won't make a graceful transition. Also, if you're dining with clients, your boss, or anyone you're trying to impress, walking out with a bag full of leftovers might not jibe with the classy image you're trying to project. Take a cue from the other people you're eating with. If no one else is taking leftovers home, you might want to leave yours, too.

Q. *Maybe it's a class or old-money thing, but I feel strange around restroom attendants. I'm not so rich or overprivileged that I need someone to hand me a paper towel or brush the lint off my clothes—I can do it myself. The problem is, if I get my own towel and don't use the hairspray or take a mint, I don't see any reason to leave a tip. Then I feel strange* and *cheap. And what if I don't have cash on me?*

A. This is a question of karma and civility, not technicalities. In addition to greeting you with a smile, a comb, and a hand towel, washroom attendants keep restrooms sparkling clean for all customers—not just the ones who pay. Chucking a buck in their basket isn't going to break the bank. If you left your purse or wallet at the table, go back and drop the tip when you're on your way out of the restaurant. Even if you choose not to use their supplies or services, think of your small tip as supporting a worthy enterprise you may desperately need some day. When you *do* need help getting out the unfortunate stain in the crotch of your pants or an emergency rescue from garlic breath, you'll be ever so grateful for their services. Remember: These are the people who will tell you when your fly is down or you have t.p. stuck to your dress shoe. Do you really want to stiff them?

Q. *We all know people who leave bad tips because they're cheap, and people who keep a running tally of a waiter's mistakes to justify shaving the tip. But I get the feeling that waiters always expect 20 percent unless something goes terribly wrong. I thought the standard tip was 10 or 15 percent, and you leave 20 percent for above-and-beyond service. What are the rules for tipping and undertipping?*

A. Everyone has their own theory and personal philosophy for tipping, but it's safe to say that at the fine dining level, where waiters are expected to be highly trained and knowledgeable about the cuisine and wine, a 15 to 20 percent tip is the norm. Most waiters in this echelon would see a 10 percent tip as a sign that something went wrong with the meal. If you didn't call attention to any problems with the food or service during the meal, the waiter will probably move on to the next reasonable conclusion, which is: You're a bad tipper.

Naturally, it makes sense to curb the tip if you endure pretentious, condescending, or rude behavior from your waiter. Likewise, it's okay to skimp if you receive poor service or bad food with no attempt to rectify the problem, no apology, and no reasonable explanation. But you should also speak up during the meal if there's a problem to give the waiter a shot at making up for it. Empty water glasses, an interminable wait for food, vanishing waiters, and mixed-up orders are all part of the regular slipups that can happen in even the best restaurants. It's how the waiter handles the problem that should dictate whether or not you undertip. If your waiter checks in to keep you informed, apologizes, and sincerely attempts to make up for any gaffs or slow service, taking your dissatisfaction out in the tip is heavy-handed. Remember that the prices on the menu cover the food—not the service. If you have a problem with what's on your plate, but not the way in which it was served, you have an issue with the kitchen, not your waiter.

BE A BUFF

Amy Vanderbilt's Complete Book of Etiquette: A Guide to Gracious Living; Letitia Baldrige's New Manners for New Times: A Complete Guide to Etiquette; How to Behave: A Guide to Modern Manners for the Socially Challenged, by Caroline Tiger

ACKNOWLEDGMENTS

For reading the early drafts and offering much-needed encouragement, I'd like to thank E. K. Buckley, Sarah Lucille Fisch, and Benjamin Rinehart.

I've always wondered about people who thank their agents, but this book would not have happened without my man, Doug Stewart, who actually took me seriously when I told him I wanted to write about food, not sex.

One of the highlights of writing this book was using the project as an excuse to call up my food and wine idols. These influential and passionate chefs, sommeliers, and restaurant insiders graciously answered my calls and enlightened this book with down-to-earth insights about the world of fine dining. Many thanks to Chef Rick Bayless, Topolobampo; Chef Homaro Cantu, Moto; Gilbert Pilgram, Chez Panisse; Chef John Folse, Chef John Folse and Company; Chef Wylie Dufresne, wd-50; general manager Tracey Spillane, Spago; Chef Scott Carsberg, Lampreia; Chef Rick Tramanto, TRU; Chef Todd Gray, Equinox; maître fromagier Max McCalman, Artisanal; Chef Peter Hoffman, Savoy; master sommelier Paul Roberts, French Laundry; master sommelier Joe Spellman, Joseph Phelps Vineyards; maître d' Arnold Chabaud, Galatoires; maître d' Alfonso De Lucia, Brasserie Jo; Frank Bismuth, Artisanal; David Rossoff, Campanile; and Susan Lifrieri, director of culinary administration, French Culinary Institute.

ABOUT THE AUTHOR

 Colleen Rush was born and raised in Louisiana, where "Didya get something to eat?" and "You hungry?" are as common a greeting as "How's your mama?" She grew up picking dewberries out of thorny ditches, catching crawfish in flooded rice fields, and learning how to make a proper roux—far, far away from the world of starched linens and gleaming silverware—and discovered very early that the best things in life always involve good food. She is a contributing writer for *Cosmopolitan* magazine, author of *Swim Naked, Defy Gravity & 99 Other Essential Things to Accomplish Before Turning 30,* and has also written for *Allure, Glamour, SELF, Shape, Redbook, Ladies' Home Journal, Maxim, Stuff, CosmoGIRL!,* and *Teen People.* She currently lives in Chicago.